Praise For Other Books By Michael W Lucas

Network Flow Analysis

"Combining a great writing style with lots of technical info, this book provides a learning experience that's both fun and interesting. Not too many technical books can claim that." -- *;login: Magazine, October 2010*

"This book is worth its weight in gold, especially if you have to deal with a shoddy ISP who always blames things on your network." — *Utahcon.com*

"The book is a comparatively quick read and will come in handy when troubleshooting and analyzing network problems." — *Mike Riley, Dr. Dobbs*

Network Flow Analysis is a pick for any library strong in network administration and data management. It's the first to show system administrators how to assess, analyze and debut a network using flow analysis, and comes form one of the best technical writers in the networking and security environments. — *Midwest Book Review*

Absolute FreeBSD, 2nd Edition

"I am happy to say that Michael Lucas is probably the best system administration author I've read. I am amazed that he can communicate top-notch content with a sense of humor, while not offending the reader or sounding stupid. When was the last time you could physically feel yourself getting smarter while reading a book? If you are a beginning to average FreeBSD user, *Absolute FreeBSD 2nd Ed* (AF2E) will deliver that sensation in spades. Even more advanced users will find plenty to enjoy." — *Richard Bejtlich, CSO, MANDIANT, and TaoSecurity blogger*

"Master practitioner Lucas organizes features and functions to make sense in the development environment, and so provides aid and comfort to new users, novices, and those with significant experience alike." — *SciTech Book News, Vol. 32, No.1*

"...reads well as the author has a very conversational tone, while giving you more than enough information on the topic at hand. He drops in jokes and honest truths, as if you were talking to him in a bar." — *Technology and Me Blog*

Cisco Routers For The Desperate, 2nd Edition

"If only *Cisco Routers for the Desperate* had been on my bookshelf a few years ago! It would have definitely saved me many hours of searching for configuration help on my Cisco routers. . . . I would strongly recommend this book for both IT Professionals looking to get started with Cisco routers, as well as anyone who has to deal with a Cisco router from time to time but doesn't have the time or technological know-how to tackle a more in-depth book on the subject." — *BLOGCRITICS MAGAZINE*

"For me, reading this book was like having one of the guys in my company who lives and breathes Cisco sitting down with me for a day and explaining everything I need to know to handle problems or issues likely to come my way. There may be many additional things I could potentially learn about my Cisco switches, but likely few I'm likely to encounter in my environment." — *IT World*

"This really ought to be the book inside every Cisco Router box for the very slim chance things go goofy and help is needed 'right now.'" — *MacCompanion*

Absolute OpenBSD

"My current favorite is *Absolute OpenBSD: Unix* for the Practical Paranoid by Michael W. Lucas from No Starch Press. Anyone should be able to read this book, download *OpenBSD*, and get it running as quickly as possible." — *Infoworld*

"I recommend *Absolute OpenBSD* to all programmers and administrators working with the OpenBSD operating system (OS), or considering it." — *UnixReview*

"*Absolute OpenBSD* by Michael Lucas is a broad and mostly gentle introduction into the world of the *OpenBSD* operating system. It is sufficiently complete and deep to give someone new to *OpenBSD* a solid footing for doing real work and the mental tools for further exploration… The potentially boring topic of systems administration is made very readable and even fun by the light tone that Lucas uses." -- *CHRIS PALMER, PRESIDENT, SAN FRANCISCO OPENBSD USERS GROUP*

PGP & GPG

"...The World's first user-friendly book on email privacy...unless you're a cryptographer, or never use email, you should read this book." — *Len Sassaman, CodeCon Founder*

"An excellent book that shows the end-user in an easy to read and often entertaining style just about everything they need to know to effectively and properly use *PGP* and *OpenPGP*." — *SLASHDOT*

"*PGP & GPG* is another excellent book by Michael Lucas. I thoroughly enjoyed his other books due to their content and style. *PGP & GPG* continues in this fine tradition. If you are trying to learn how to use PGP or GPG, or at least want to ensure you are using them properly, read *PGP & GPG*." — *TAOSECURITY,*

SSH Mastery

OpenSSH, PuTTY, Tunnels and Keys

by Michael W Lucas

Author: Michael W Lucas

Copyeditor: Aidan Julianna "AJ" Powell

Cover: Bradley K McDevitt

Layout: Jessica McDevitt

Published by Tilted Windmill Press in January 2012.

For information on book distribution or translations, please contact Tilted Windmill Press (http://www.tiltedwindmillpress.com).

And as always, this one is for Liz.

Contents

Detailed Contents

Acknowledgments

Thanks to the folks who wrote OpenSSH and PuTTY in the first place, and those who encouraged me to write this book.

A special thanks to my technical reviewers: Chris Buechler, Jez Caudle, Sean Cody, Daniel Čižinský, James E Keenan, Alexander Leidinger, Brett Mahar, Philipp Marek, Glen Matthews, Damien Miller, Scott Murphy, Mike O'Connor, Phil Pennock, Amanda Robinson, George Rosamond, Richard Toohey, and Giovanni Torres. Any errors in this book crept in despite the efforts of these fine folks.

I would also like to thank iX Systems (http://www.ixsystems.com/). Writing SSH Mastery would have been vastly more annoying without their assistance.

Chapter 1:
Introducing OpenSSH

Over the last ten years, OpenSSH (http://www.openssh.com) has become the standard tool for remote management of Unix-like systems and many network devices. Most systems administrators use only the bare minimum OpenSSH functionality necessary to get a command line, however. OpenSSH has many powerful features that will make systems management easier if you take the time to learn about them. You'll find information and tutorials about OpenSSH all over the Internet. Some of them are poorly written, or only applicable to very specific scenarios. Many are well-written, but are ten years old and cover problems solved by a software update nine years ago. If you have a few spare days, and know the questions to ask, you can sift through the dross and find effective, current tutorials.

This task-oriented book will save you that effort and time, freeing you up to prepare for the next version of Skyrim. I assume that you are using fairly recent versions of OpenSSH and PuTTY, and disregard edge cases such as "my 12-year-old router only supports SSH version 1." If you found this book, chances are you're capable of searching the Internet to answer very specific questions. I won't discuss building OpenSSH from source, or how to install the OpenSSH server on fifty different platforms. If you are a systems administrator, you know where to find that information. If you are a systems user, your systems administrator should install and configure the OpenSSH server for you, but you can still master the client programs.

Who Should Read This Book?

Everyone who manages a UNIX-like system must understand SSH. OpenSSH is the most commonly deployed SSH implementation. Unless you're specifically using a different SSH implementation, read this book.

People who are not systems administrators, but who must connect to a server over SSH, will also find this book helpful. While you can learn the basics of SSH in five minutes, proper SSH use will make your job easier and faster. You can skip the sections on server configuration if you wish.

What is SSH?

Secure Shell (SSH) is a protocol for creating an encrypted communications channel between two networked hosts. SSH protects data passing between two machines so that other people cannot eavesdrop on it. Tatu Ylönen created the initial protocol and implementation in 1995, and it quickly spread to replace insecure protocols such as telnet, rsh, and rlogin. Today, many different software packages rely on the SSH protocol for encrypted and well-authenticated transport of data across private, public, and hostile networks.

What is OpenSSH?

OpenSSH is the most widely deployed implementation of the SSH protocol. It started as an offshoot of a freely-licensed version of the original SSH software, but has been heavily rewritten, expanded, and updated. OpenSSH is developed by the OpenBSD Project, a team known for writing secure software. OpenSSH is the standard SSH implementation in the Linux and BSD world, and is also used in products from large companies such as HP, Cisco, Oracle, Novell, Dell, Juniper, IBM, and so on.

OpenSSH comes in two versions, *OpenBSD* and *Portable OpenSSH*. OpenSSH's main development happens as part of OpenBSD. This version of OpenSSH is small and secure, but only supports OpenBSD. The OpenSSH Portability Team takes the OpenBSD version and adds the glue necessary to make OpenSSH work on other operating systems, creating Portable OpenSSH. Not only do different operating systems use different compilers, libraries, and so on, but they have very different authentication systems. This book applies to both versions.

Any non-Microsoft operating system probably comes with OpenSSH, or the operating system vendor provides a package. If not, download the Portable OpenSSH source code from http://www.OpenSSH.org/ and follow the instructions to build the software.

OpenSSH is available under a BSD-style license. You can use it for any purpose, with no strings attached. You cannot sue the software authors if OpenSSH breaks and you can't claim you wrote OpenSSH, but you can use it in any way you wish, including adding it to your own products. You can charge to install or support OpenSSH, but the software itself is free.

SSH Server

An SSH server listens on the network for incoming SSH requests, authenticates those requests, and provides a system command prompt (or another service that you configure). The most popular SSH server is OpenSSH's `sshd`.

SSH Clients

You use an SSH client to connect to your remote server or network device. The most popular SSH client for Windows systems is *PuTTY*, while the standard SSH client for Unix-like systems is *ssh*, from OpenSSH. Both clients are freely available and usable for any purpose, commercial or noncommercial, at no cost. We'll cover both.

SSH Protocol Versions

The SSH protocol comes in two versions, SSH-1 (version 1) and SSH-2 (version 2). ***Always use SSH-2***. Verifying that your server only speaks SSH-2 requires checking a single entry (*Protocol*) in the SSH server configuration, as discussed in Chapter 3. If you promise to do that, you can skip the rest of section.

One person designed the original SSH protocol for his own needs, and it met those needs admirably. As SSH grew more popular and more people tried to break it, the protocol required revision. SSH-1 is vulnerable to attacks. While SSH-1 will encrypt your data in transit and prevent casual eavesdropping, a knowledgeable attacker can capture your data, decrypt your data in transit, fool you into thinking that you logged onto the correct machine when you are actually connected to a different machine, insert arbitrary text into the data stream, or any combination of these. Attacking an SSH-1 data stream isn't quite a point-and-click process, but intruders do break SSH-1 in the real world. The appearance of security is worse than no security. ***Do not use SSH version 1***.

It might seem harmless to permit SSH-1 for servers or clients that don't support SSH-2. The client and server negotiate the SSH version they will use, however. If either client or server accepts SSH version 1 an intruder can hijack the connection, letting him capture your login credentials and all data you transmit. It's fairly straightforward to insert arbitrary text (such as `rm -rf /*`) into an SSH-1 session. This was discovered in

1998, and increases in computing power have only made the attack easier. Worst of all, version 1 sessions can now be decoded in real time by programs such as Ettercap. Developers have added defenses into SSH-1, but they are not guaranteed to protect you. Do not let your SSH clients request SSH-1. Do not let your OpenSSH servers offer SSH-1.

You'll see references to several upgrades to SSH-1, such as SSH version 1.3 and 1.5. These modifications to version 1 are vulnerable. Do not use them. SSH servers that offer SSH version 1.99 support SSH version 1 and version 2. Clients that can only speak SSH version 1 can connect to these servers, but clients capable of SSH version 2 will use the later protocol. SSH version 1.99 is just as vulnerable as any other SSH-1.

SSH-2 is the modern standard. There are no known security problems with the protocol, and the protocol is designed so that most vulnerabilities can be quickly addressed. Increasing computing power makes today's unfeasible attacks possible tomorrow, so SSH-2 is designed such that security flaws can be addressed without replacing the entire protocol.

Protocols such as SCP and SFTP (Chapter 6) are actually built atop both SSH protocols. And both SSH protocol versions include sub-protocols for authentication, encryption, and transport. SSH-2 supports everything in SSH-1 and more.

What Isn't In This Book?

This book is meant to get you to use the OpenSSH and PuTTY varieties of SSH with a minimum level of security and professional competence. This means eliminating passwords and restricting your SSH services to the minimum necessary privileges. You will be able to easily copy files over SSH. You'll manage server keys with a minimum of fuss.

This book is not intended to be a comprehensive SSH tome. I don't cover integrating SSH with Kerberos, or SecureID, or hooking your SSH install into Google Authentication, or attaching sudo to your SSH agent. These are all interesting topics, but very platform-specific, and might well change before you finish reading this book.

What Is In This Book?

Chapter 1 is this introduction.

Chapter 2, "Encryption and Keys," gives basic information about encryption and how SSH uses encryption.

Chapter 3, "The OpenSSH Server," discusses configuring the OpenSSH server `sshd`. While this chapter covers basic configuration, more specific examples will appear throughout the rest of the book.

Chapter 4, "Host Key Verification," covers a frequently overlooked but vital part of using any SSH client: verifying host keys. This topic is so important that it gets its own chapter, even before SSH clients.

Chapter 5, "SSH Clients," discusses the two standard SSH clients, OpenSSH's `ssh` and PuTTY.

Chapter 6, "Copying Files over SSH," covers moving files across the network with the tools `scp` (secure copy) and `sftp` (SSH file transfer).

Chapter 7, "SSH Keys," walks you through creating a personal key pair (public and private cryptographic key). Key pairs make authentication more secure. When combined with agents, they eliminate the need to routinely type passwords but don't degrade SSH security.

Chapter 8, "X Forwarding," will teach you how to display graphics over your SSH connection while minimizing risk.

Chapter 9, "Port Forwarding," covers using OpenSSH as a generic TCP/IP proxy, letting you redirect arbitrary network connections through the network to remote machines.

Chapter 10, "Keeping SSH Sessions Open," covers ways to keep OpenSSH sessions running despite the firewalls and proxy servers that want to shut them down after minutes or hours.

Chapter 11, "Host Key Distribution," tells systems administrators how to automatically distribute host keys and improve security while eliminating the need for users to manually compare server key fingerprints.

Chapter 12, "Limiting SSH," discusses ways to use SSH encryption behind automated tools and tightly-controlled user tasks as well as creating single-purpose user keys.

Chapter 13, "OpenSSH VPNs," demonstrates how to use OpenSSH to create an encrypted tunnel between two sites.

Enough blather! Let's get to work.

Chapter 2:
Encryption, Algorithms, and Keys

OpenSSH encrypts traffic. What does that mean, and how does it work? For a longer explanation check my book "PGP & GPG," but here's the brief summary:

Encryption transforms readable plain text into unreadable *ciphertext* that attackers cannot understand. *Decryption* reverses the transformation, producing readable text from apparent gibberish. An *encryption algorithm* is the exact method for performing this transformation. Most children discover the code that substitutes numbers for letters, so that A=1, B=2, Z=26, and so on. This is a simple encryption algorithm. Modern computer-driven encryption algorithms work on chunks of text at a time and perform far more complicated transformations.

Most encryption algorithms use a *key*; a chunk of text, numbers, symbols, or data used to encrypt messages. The key can be chosen by the user or randomly generated. (People habitually choose easily-guessed keys, so I strongly recommend random generation.) The encryption algorithm uses the key to encrypt the text, making it more difficult for an outsider to decrypt. Even if you know the encryption algorithm, you cannot decrypt the message without the secret encryption key.

Think of an encryption algorithm as a type of lock, and the key as a specific key. Locks come in many different types: house doors, bicycles, factories, and so on. Each uses a certain type of key – your door key is probably the wrong shape to fit into any vehicle ignition. But a key of the proper type still won't work in the wrong lock. Your front door key unlocks your front door, and only your front door. Encryption keys work similarly.

Algorithm Types

Encryption algorithms come in two varieties, symmetric and asymmetric.

A *symmetric algorithm* uses the same key for both encryption and decryption. Symmetric algorithms include but are not limited to the Advanced Encryption Standard (AES), Blowfish, 3DES, and IDEA. The child's substitution code is a symmetric algorithm. Once you know that A=1 and so on, you can encrypt and decrypt messages. Symmetric algorithms (more sophisticated than simple substitution) can be very fast and secure, so long as only authorized people have the key. And that's the problem: an outsider who gets the key can read your messages or replace them with his own. You must protect the key. Sending the key unencrypted across the Internet is like standing on the playground shouting "A is 1, B is 2." Anyone who hears the key can read your private message.

An *asymmetric algorithm* uses different keys for encryption and decryption. You encrypt a message with one key, and then decrypt it with another. This works because the keys are very large numbers, and very large numbers behave oddly when multiplied together. (There are very good explanations out on the Internet, if you want the details.) Asymmetric encryption became popular only with the wide availability of computers that can handle the very difficult math, and is much, much slower and more computationally expensive than symmetric encryption.

Having two separate keys creates interesting possibilities. Make one key public. Give it away. Broadcast it to the entire world. Keep the other key very private, and protect it at all costs. Anyone who has the public key can encrypt a message that only the private key holder can read. Someone who has the private key can encrypt a message and send it out into the world. Anyone can use the public key to decrypt that message, but the fact that the public key can decrypt the message assures recipients that the message sender had the private key. This is the basis of *public key encryption*. The public key and its matching private key are called a *key pair*. Again, think of the lock on your front door. The lock itself is public; anyone can touch it. The key is private. You must have both to get into your home. (If you want more detail, research "Diffie-Hellman key exchange.")

How SSH Uses Encryption

Symmetric encryption is fast, but offers no way for hosts to securely exchange keys. Asymmetric encryption lets hosts exchange public keys, but it's slow and computationally expensive. But how can you efficiently encrypt a session between two hosts that have never previously communicated?

Every SSH server has a key pair. Whenever a client connects, the server and the client use this key pair to negotiate a temporary key pair shared only between those two hosts. The client and the server both use this temporary key to derive a symmetric key that they will use to exchange data during this session, as well as related keys to provide connection integrity. If the session runs for a long time or exchanges a lot of data, the computers will intermittently negotiate a new temporary key pair and a new symmetric key. The SSH protocol is more complicated than this, and includes safeguards to prevent many different cryptographic attacks, but cryptographic key exchange is the heart of the protocol.

SSH supports many symmetric and asymmetric encryption algorithms. The client and server negotiate mutually agreeable algorithms at every connection. While OpenSSH offers options to easily change the algorithms supported and its preference for each, don't! People infinitely more knowledgeable about encryption than you or I, and with more encryption experience than both of us together, arrived at OpenSSH's encryption preferences after much hard thought and troubleshooting. Gossip, rumor, and innuendo might crown Blowfish as the awesome encryption algorithm *du jour*, but that doesn't mean you should tweak your OpenSSH server to use that algorithm and no other.

The most common reason people offer for changing the encryption algorithms is to improve speed. SSH's primary purpose is security, not speed. Do not abandon security to improve speed.

Now that you understand how SSH encryption works, leave the encryption settings alone.

Chapter 3:
The OpenSSH Server

The OpenSSH server *sshd* is highly configurable and lets you restrict who may connect to the server, what actions those users can take, and what actions it will permit. In this chapter, I assume that OpenSSH has been installed as part of your base operating system, with the server program in */usr/sbin*. Your operating system might differ.

Test if `sshd` is listening to the network with the telnet command. Here, I connect to the host avarice on the standard SSH port, 22.

```
$ telnet avarice 22
Trying 192.0.2.8...
Connected to avarice.
Escape character is '^]'.
SSH-2.0-OpenSSH_5.6
^]
telnet> c
```

The host is listening on port 22. When you connect over raw TCP, sshd returns an SSH banner. If you don't get something similar, sshd isn't running (or perhaps something on the network is blocking your connection; check your firewall). Immediately upon connection, the server announces the supported version of the SSH protocol (SSH-2.0) and the server program and version (OpenSSH 5.6). Hit CTRL-] to escape to the telnet prompt, and then c and ENTER to close the connection.

Additionally, you should see sshd in the server's process list.

```
$ ps ax | grep sshd
❶ 24405 ?? Is 0:00.03 /usr/sbin/sshd
❷ 4062 ?? Is 0:00.04 sshd: mwlucas [priv] (sshd)
❸ 6385 ?? S 0:00.01 sshd: mwlucas@ttypB (sshd)
```

This server runs `sshd` as ❶ process 24405. The second `sshd` entry is for the ❷ privileged `sshd` process required for every SSH session, while the third is the ❸ unprivileged SSH session I'm actively using. (If someone has deliberately disabled `sshd`'s privilege separation and is running sshd insecurely, you won't see the unprivileged session.) Most operating systems run sshd as a standalone server without any command-line arguments. The most common way to manage `sshd`'s behavior is with the configuration file, */etc/ssh/sshd_config*. Before you start mucking with those settings, though, you should know how to test and debug changes.

Testing and Debugging sshd

OpenSSH makes debugging sshd configurations as simple as possible. You must be root to debug sshd. The simplest debugging methods are alternate configuration files, alternate ports, and debugging mode.

Alternate Configurations and Ports

The -f command-line argument tells sshd to use an alternate configuration file. Here I tell sshd to use a test configuration.

```
# /usr/sbin/sshd -f sshd_config.test
```

Note that I executed sshd by the full path. sshd needs a full path so it can re-execute itself when accepting a connection.

Only one sshd instance can attach to a particular TCP port on a given IP address. Your test sshd process cannot start because it cannot bind port 22. You could edit *sshd_config.test* to assign your test process another port, but it's simpler to use an alternate port with the -p command-line argument.

```
# /usr/sbin/sshd -f sshd_config.test -p 2022
```

Your test instance is now listening on TCP port 2022. (Note that a *ListenAddress* keyword binding sshd to a port overrides a command-line -p; see "Configuring sshd" later this chapter.)

By setting an alternate configuration file and port on the command line, you make only the config file changes you want to test. Once you know your new configuration works, you can copy the test configuration to /etc/ssh/sshd_config and restart the main system sshd process, confident that you didn't break anything. (Not that I've ever broken the system by testing, mind you.) I recommend saving your original *sshd_config*, preferably with some sort of version control, just in case your change causes problems you don't immediately notice.

Remember to kill your test sshd process when finished testing.

Debugging sshd

The -d flag tells sshd to run in debugging mode, without detaching from the controlling terminal. Debugging displays everything your sshd process does as it happens. Here I run sshd with debugging.

```
# /usr/sbin/sshd -f sshd_config -p 2022 -d
debug1: sshd version OpenSSH_5.6 ❶
debug1: read PEM private key done: type RSA ❷
debug1: private host key: #0 type 1 RSA
debug1: read PEM private key done: type DSA
debug1: private host key: #1 type 2 DSA
debug1: read PEM private key done: type ECDSA
debug1: private host key: #2 type 3 ECDSA
debug1: rexec_argv[0]='/usr/sbin/sshd' ❸
debug1: rexec_argv[1]='-f'
debug1: rexec_argv[2]='sshd_config'
debug1: rexec_argv[3]='-p'
debug1: rexec_argv[4]='2022'
debug1: rexec_argv[5]='-d'
debug1: Bind to port 2022 on ::. ❹
Server listening on :: port 2022. ❺
debug1: Bind to port 2022 on 0.0.0.0.
Server listening on 0.0.0.0 port 2022.
```

The debug session shows the ❶ OpenSSH version you're running. You then see sshd ❷ read the server's private keys as specified in *sshd_config* and ❸ parse the command-line arguments and options. It ❹ attempts to bind to your chosen IPv6 TCP port, ❺ reports success, and repeats the process for IPv4. The server is now running and ready to accept connections.

If you attempt to connect to this server with an SSH client, the server will display more debugging output. (An OpenSSH server in debugging mode will not fork, so it can only accept one client connection at a time.) sshd prints every action taken as server and client offer each other encryption algorithms and keys, the user attempts to authenticate, and various SSH features like X11 forwarding are negotiated. I won't walk you through such a session, as the output varies widely depending on the client, the authentication method, and the SSH features requested and offered. If you have a problem with your SSH server, run it in debugging mode on a different port and read the output. sshd frequently states problems in plain language. If you don't understand the error message, use it as an Internet search term.

When you finish debugging, exit out of your client and the sshd process will end. You can also hit CTRL-C in the sshd terminal, unceremoniously terminating `sshd` and disconnecting the client.

   `sshd` can also run in quiet mode with the `-q` command-line option. In quiet mode, `sshd` doesn't send messages to the system log when a user logs in, authenticates, or logs out. You want to be able to identify who logged into your production systems so quiet mode isn't useful on live servers, but `-q` might help in special debugging situations. Try it and see.

   If `-d` doesn't provide enough detail, add more `-d`'s to increase verbosity. Running `/usr/sbin/sshd -ddddd` should satisfy your curiosity in delightful detail.

Configuring sshd

All system-wide `sshd` (and client) configuration files reside in `/etc/ssh` by default. Some operating systems use an alternate location – for example, Darwin puts the SSH configuration files directly in `/etc`, while OSX uses `/private`. The standard files are:

   ⅄ `ssh_config` – the system-wide OpenSSH client configuration (see Chapter 5)
   ⅄ `ssh_host_*_key` – the server's private keys, in various encryption algorithms
   ⅄ `ssh_host_*_key.pub` – the server's public keys, corresponding to the private keys using the same algorithms
   ⅄ `sshd_config` – the OpenSSH server configuration

   While you can tweak `sshd` with command-line options, permanent configuration is generally handled in the configuration file. The configuration is a set of keywords and values, as shown in this snippet.

```
#Port 22 ❶
#AddressFamily any ❷
#ListenAddress 0.0.0.0 ❸
#ListenAddress :: ❹
# The default requires explicit activation of protocol 1
#Protocol 2
...
```

   We'll cover the function of each configuration option later; for now, just understand how the file is laid out.

   The pound sign (#) indicates a comment. Everything after that is ignored. The OpenSSH team distributes `sshd_config` with options set to the defaults, all commented out. `sshd` can run just fine with everything at the default setting. To change the defaults, remove the pound sign and change the value. For example, the configuration option ❶ Port is set to 22, ❷ AddressFamily is set to any, and ListenAddress is set to both ❸ 0.0.0.0 (all IPv4 addresses on the local machine) and ❹ :: (all IPv6 addresses on the local machine). These are defaults, and commented out. The rest of *sshd_config* follows this keyword/value format.

I'll give some generally useful sshd options in this chapter. Most *sshd_config* options appear in the sections where they're most relevant. For example, sshd options affecting X11 forwarding appear in Chapter 9. If you want the comprehensive master list of *sshd_config* keywords, read the *sshd_config* manual page.

Not all currently-deployed versions of OpenSSH support all the keywords described in this chapter. I've written this based on the most recent OpenSSH. Some operating systems either include older versions, or deliberately remove certain functions for their own reasons. If a configuration option doesn't work on your server, consult your operating system documentation or ask your vendor.

Set Host Keys

The HostKey keyword gives the full path to a file containing a private key.

```
# HostKey for protocol version 1
#HostKey /etc/ssh/ssh_host_key
# HostKeys for protocol version 2
#HostKey /etc/ssh/ssh_host_rsa_key
#HostKey /etc/ssh/ssh_host_dsa_key
#HostKey /etc/ssh/ssh_host_ecdsa_key
```

For your sanity, the default files are named after the type of key they normally contain. The file *ssh_host_rsa_key* contains an RSA key, *ssh_host_ecdsa_key* is an ECDSA key, and so on. This isn't mandatory – OpenSSH will figure out what type of key is in a file and load it if appropriate – but it's definitely best practice.

Operating systems handle missing key files differently. BSD-based and Red Hat systems usually create missing default key files automatically. Many Linux systems require the systems administrator to manually create missing key files, but use a familiar tool to create them. For example, Debian-based systems create missing key files when you run **dpkg-reconfigure openssh-server**.

Chapter 7 covers creating host keys by hand.

Network Options

sshd lets you control which network protocols it uses, the addresses it uses, and the TCP port it attaches to.

```
#Port 22
#AddressFamily any
#ListenAddress 0.0.0.0
#ListenAddress ::
```

The *Port* keyword controls the TCP port. 22 is the standard port defined for SSH. Some organizations use a different port for SSH in the hope of improving security. Running SSH on an unusual port won't actually help secure SSH, but it will reduce the number of login attempts from SSH-cracking worms. You can override the Port keyword on the command line with -p (see "Testing and Debugging sshd" earlier this chapter).

AddressFamily refers to the versions of TCP/IP sshd uses. To only use IPv4, set this to *inet*. To only use IPv6, set this to *inet6*. The default, *any*, uses either version.

Many hosts have multiple IP addresses. By default, sshd listens for incoming requests on all of them. If you want limit the IP addresses that sshd attaches to, use the *ListenAddress* keyword. Each ListenAddress keyword takes a single IP address as an argument, but you can use as many ListenAddress keywords as necessary. Explicitly list every IP address that you want the SSH server to accept connections on.

If a host has many IP addresses and you want to block SSH access to just a few of them, you might find blocking traffic with a packet filter easier than using many ListenAddress statements.

You can also use ListenAddress to define extra ports for sshd to listen on. If your host has three IP addresses, and you want sshd to listen to different ports on each, use ListenAddress statements.

```
ListenAddress 192.0.2.8:22
ListenAddress 192.0.2.9:25
ListenAddress 192.0.2.10:80
```

Three addresses, with three different ports. Mind you, having sshd listen to the SMTP and HTTP ports is generally unwise, but OpenSSH is not designed to prevent you from doing unwise things. If you're stuck behind a packet filter that only allows outgoing connections to port 80, running sshd on port 80 would let you evade the firewall. (The impact of evading the corporate firewall on your employment is left as an exercise for the reader.)

SSH Protocol Version

Always use SSH protocol version 2. Do not use SSH-1.

```
Protocol 2
```

If you cannot beg, batter, belabor, blackmail, or bludgeon your way out of offering SSH-1, `sshd` will support you. The order doesn't matter, because the client will select the version it prefers from what the server offers.

```
Protocol 2,1
```

SSH-1 permits man-in-the-middle attacks and session hijacking, as discussed in Chapter 1. If someone insists on using SSH-1, practice saying "I told you so."

Banners and Login Messages

Many administrators want to display a message to the user before they log in. This is called a *banner*. Banners don't always work, however, depending on exactly how the client connects. You can create a file containing a banner message and set the keyword Banner to the full path of the file, but be aware that it won't always appear.

```
Banner /etc/ssh/ssh-banner
```

The SSH protocol does not guarantee banner display before clients authenticate.

You can reliably display the system message of the day, `/etc/motd`. This message does not appear until after the client has authenticated, so it might not meet your needs. The *PrintMotd* keyword can be *yes* or *no*.

```
PrintMotd yes
```

Be aware that if the banner works, it might interfere with automated processes run over SSH. In some locations, though, a banner message can serve as legal notice to intruders. Choose the headache you prefer.

On systems that use Pluggable Authentication Modules (PAM), a PAM module can print `/etc/motd`. If you're having trouble controlling the display of `/etc/motd`, check your PAM configuration.

Once a user has logged on, `sshd` prints the time of the user's last logon and where they logged in from. If you want to turn this off, you can set *PrintLastLog* to *no*.

```
PrintLastLog yes
```

I recommend leaving this on. More than once, users have alerted me to intrusions when they logged in and saw that their previous login was from a foreign country or at a ridiculous hour.

Authentication Options

By default, a user can try to log in 6 times in 2 minutes in a single session. Twenty seconds should be long enough for most people to type their password correctly, but you can control the length of time and how many times the user can try.

The *LoginGraceTime* keyword controls how much time sshd gives a user to authenticate. If a user is connected to sshd for this time without successfully authenticating, the connection is terminated. This takes a number of seconds(s), minutes(m), or hours(h).

```
LoginGraceTime 2m
```

You can also control how many times a user may attempt to authenticate in a single connection with *MaxAuthTries*. The default is 6.

```
MaxAuthTries 6
```

After half of a user's permitted attempts in a single session have failed, the system logs further failures. Authentication attempts include both public key authentication and passwords. After MaxAuthTries failures, the user must initiate a new SSH session to try again. (My usual failure procedure is to fail to log in six times, then remember that I have a different username on this machine. When I follow my own advice on changing usernames from Chapter 5, and install a public key everywhere as in Chapter 7, I don't have this problem.)

Verifying Login Attempts against DNS

The owner of an IP address controls the reverse DNS for that address. By default, sshd uses reverse DNS to generate log messages. A log message like "Login failed from secretary's computer" will make you sigh. A log message like "Login failed from Hacker Haven Nation" should trigger an alarm. An intruder who controls the reverse DNS for his IP address can change the apparent hostname to something within your company. For protection against this sort of attack, sshd can verify connection attempts against DNS entries.

```
UseDNS yes
```

UseDNS verifies the forward and reverse DNS names for a client's IP address. When a client connects, `sshd` looks up the host name for the source IP, then looks up the IP address for that host name. If the DNS names don't match, the connection will be rejected.

Suppose an intruder controls the reverse DNS for his IP address 192.0.2.99. He gives it a hostname within your company, such as **desktop9.blackhelicopters.org**, and connects to your SSH server. Your SSH server will ask its DNS server for the IP address for **desktop9.blackhelicopters.org**. If the DNS entry for that hostname doesn't match the IP the connection is coming from, the connection will be rejected. While an intruder might control the reverse DNS of his own IP address, he probably doesn't control the forward DNS of your domain. (If he does, get him out of your systems, secure them, and disable SSH passwords as discussed in Chapter 7.)

DNS checks also don't help if the intruder can poison the server's DNS cache. Also, DNS checks can increase system load. The additional load for any one session is small, but if you serve hundreds or thousands of SSH users, DNS checks just might topple the system. And when the DNS server is down, failed DNS checks will slow down all SSH logins.

Finally, many IPv6 sites haven't configured reverse DNS and will be slow for the foreseeable future.

Disable DNS checking by setting UseDNS to *no*.

System Administration Features

Tell `sshd` where to stash its process ID file with the *PidFile* keyword in *sshd_config*.

```
PidFile /var/run/sshd.pid
```

This file is written before `sshd` reduces its privileges, so it and the directory it's in don't require special permissions.

OpenSSH `sshd` uses syslog for logging, defaulting to the AUTH facility and the INFO level. Control these with the SyslogFacility and LogLevel keywords.

```
SyslogFacility AUTH
LogLevel INFO
```

The SyslogFacility keyword accepts any valid syslog facility. Below is a list of accepted LogLevel values and what they send to syslogd.

⅄ QUIET: logs nothing

⅄ FATAL: when sshd dies

⅄ ERROR: only problems

⅄ INFO: standard login/logoff messages

⅄ VERBOSE: every detail that doesn't violate privacy, including the fingerprints of public keys used to authenticate

⅄ DEBUG1, DEBUG2, DEBUG3: These log enough data to violate user privacy. Debug messages are sent to syslog. Most default syslog installations don't capture this level of detail; you'll need to configure your syslog server to capture all debugging data for this to be useful.

The defaults fit almost all environments.

Changing Encryption Algorithms

You might find the keywords *Cipher* and *Mac* in your configuration. (They don't appear in the sshd_config provided by OpenSSH, but some operating systems add them.) These settings allow you to change the encryption methods your server supports. Don't muck with these settings. You will only hurt yourself.

Restricting Access by User or Group

I know of many applications – mainly industrial and business programs – that make use of user accounts from the underlying operating system. People use the application over a Web page or proprietary client, but never actually log on to the operating system. If Fred down in shipping needs to access the application, the system needs a **fred** account. (This isn't ideal practice, but it is reality.) If you're responsible for such an application, configure your system so that users who are not systems administrators cannot log on to the server. OpenSSH supports this with the *DenyUsers*, *AllowUsers*, *DenyGroups*, and *AllowGroups* options. These options take comma-delimited lists of users or groups as arguments, and are processed in the order listed in the configuration file on a first-match basis.

- If a user is listed in DenyUsers, he cannot log in via SSH. As the directives are processed in order, a user listed here will be prevented from logging in even if he is listed in AllowUsers or is a member of a group in AllowGroups. This lets you make exceptions for individual users in a group.

- If a user is listed in AllowUsers he can log in via SSH, even if he is a member of a group in a DenyGroups entry.

- If a user is in a group listed in DenyGroups, he cannot log in via SSH. Override this by listing the user in AllowUsers.

- If a user is in a group listed in AllowGroups, he can log in via SSH. Both DenyUsers and DenyGroups overrides this.

Additionally, the presence of an AllowUsers or AllowGroups entry implies that nobody else can log in. The system denies SSH logins to all users who are not in one of these.

Confused? Let's look at some examples. My system has four users: **backup, mwlucas, pkdick**, and **jgballard**. They are in groups as below:

```
wheel: mwlucas
staff: mwlucas, pkdick, jgballard
support: pkdick, mwlucas
billing: jgballard
```

While these are small groups, the principles apply to groups with any number of users.

The billing application requires system accounts, but the user doesn't need access via SSH. If I just want to block the billing user from SSH, I could use DenyUsers.

```
DenyUsers jgballard
```

All users not listed would still have SSH access. When I add another billing user, though, I must explicitly list them in DenyUsers. I'm better served by blocking access by group.

On a BSD system, *wheel* is the group for systems administrators. (Ubuntu does something similar with sudo and the "admin" group.) To allow only systems administrators to log in, use the following configuration.

```
AllowGroups wheel
```

Anyone in the wheel group can log in. The presence of an Allow-Groups entry tells sshd that it should deny logins by default. The users pkdick and jgballard cannot SSH in.

I could do something similar by listing mwlucas explicitly.

```
AllowUsers mwlucas
```

The problem with this is that when I get another systems administrator, I must add him to the wheel group and edit *sshd_config*. I'm likely to forget one or the other. Whenever possible, use groups.

My users are globally distributed and synchronized via LDAP. While my support team has access to most of my systems, I have one particular system where a certain administrator is forbidden to log in. Here I block that user, but permit the group.

```
DenyUsers pkdick
AllowGroups support
```

Some applications, such as properly-configured `rsync`, need accounts with SSH access. This requires a user account with public key authentication (see Chapter 7). These accounts can be dangerous. While you can restrict the commands that can be run after authenticating with a public key, you don't want rsync connections from random hosts, and you don't want a user with shell access able to circumvent restrictions by editing a file he owns. You can use the Allow and Deny options to restrict where users can connect from by adding an @ and a host or IP address after the username. List hosts by IP or hostname. Hostnames are verified with reverse DNS, so using hostnames carries the usual security problems. Here I restrict one user's access.

```
AllowUsers backup@192.0.2.0/25
AllowGroups support
```

Users in the support group can log in from anywhere, and the user backup can log in from any host with an IP between 192.0.2.0 and 192.0.2.127. All other users are denied.

With sensible group memberships and proper Allow and Deny options, you can restrict login access as needed. When in doubt, give accounts the least level of privileges that will let users and programs accomplish their required tasks.

Wildcards in OpenSSH Configuration Files

The configuration files for the OpenSSH server and client accept wildcards, called *patterns*. Rather than listing all possible IP addresses in a network, patterns let you say "anything that matches this expression." Wildcards are used for Match rules (see "Conditional Configuration with Match," later this chapter) and in `ssh_config` (see Chapter 5). Patterns let you write OpenSSH rules such as "all hosts in this domain" or "all IP addresses in this network." The two wildcard characters are:

```
? matches exactly one character
* matches zero or more characters
```

For example, I could write a pattern indicating any host in blackhelicopters.org.

```
Host *.blackhelicopters.org
```

I must use the asterisk wild card, because one question mark matches exactly one character.

The next pattern matches all hosts in the blackhelicopters.org domain that have five-character hostnames. It matches **sloth.blackhelicopters.org**, but not **gluttony.blackhelicopters.org** or **avarice.blackhelicopters.org**.

```
Host ?????.blackhelicopters.org
```

We can use patterns for IP addresses as well. Here I match the hosts 192.0.2.10 through 192.0.2.19.

```
Address 192.0.2.1?
```

To match any host in 192.0.2.0/24, you can use an asterisk. The next pattern matches any address from 192.0.2.0 through 192.0.2.255.

```
Address 192.0.2.*
```

For IP addresses, you can also use actual netmasks.

```
Address 192.0.2.0/26, 192.0.2.192/26
```

Note that we used multiple IP addresses, separated with a comma. Most configuration options accept lists of patterns like this. (The Host option is slightly different, in that terms are separated by a white space. We'll go through several examples of per-host configuration in Chapter 5.)

We can negate patterns by putting an exclamation point in front. The next pattern excludes the hosts in blackhelicopters.org.

```
Host !*.blackhelicopters.org
```

Negation is most useful when combined with a larger entity – that is, to say "Match everything except that one little piece." If I want to match every host in blackhelicopters.org except for the customers in the subdomain vermin.blackhelicopters.org, I could use this pattern. The lead OpenSSH developer describes negation as "a little fiddly," so you might have trouble with it. Negation isn't supported everywhere; you'll have to try it and see if it works in your environment.

```
Host !*.vermin.blackhelicopters.org *.blackhelicopters.org
```

We'll make use of patterns throughout configuring the OpenSSH server and client.

Conditional Configuration with Match

Your server might need to behave differently depending on the source address or hostname of an incoming connection, or the username, or even what groups a user belongs to. Some users might require chroot (see "Chrooting Users" later this chapter), or perhaps particular users may use X11 forwarding (Chapter 9) from the local LAN. The *Match* keyword lets you set special sshd configurations for these situations.
A Match statement is followed by a set of conditions, then by a series of configuration statements `sshd` should apply to connections that meet all of those conditions.

Before implementing a Match statement, configure `sshd` for the most common situation. You might want to deny X11 forwarding to all but select users. Configure `sshd` to deny X11 forwarding, then use a Match statement to check the username and permit X11 forwarding. While we haven't covered X11 forwarding yet, denying it is a single entry in *sshd_config*:

```
X11Forwarding no
```

In all of the examples below, assume this entry appears near the beginning of *sshd_config*.

Matching Users and Groups

The most common situation I encounter is when I want to enable an option for a particular user or group. The User or Group Match terms permit this.

```
Match User mwlucas
    X11Forwarding yes
```

I am always permitted to use X11 forwarding, as my awesome psychic powers eliminate all possible security risks.

If all of my systems administrators share these powers, or if I settle for exterminating sysadmins who empower intruders, I could Match the whole group.

```
Match Group wheel
        X11Forwarding yes
```

If you need multiple Match terms, separate them by commas.

```
Match User mwlucas,jgballard
        X11Forwarding yes
```

I know when to use X11 forwarding. My user claims he does, too. We'll see.

Matching Addresses or Hosts

Perhaps you must permit X11 forwarding, but only from particular networks. You can Match on IP addresses or hostnames.

```
Match Address 192.0.2.0/29, 192.0.2.128/27
        X11Forwarding yes
```

Similarly, Match accepts hostnames, with the usual DNS security caveats.

```
Match Host *.blackhelicopters.org, *.openssh.org
        X11Forwarding yes
```

Multiple Match Conditions

You can list multiple Match terms on a single line. Here, we permit a single user to use password authentication if they connect from a specific IP address.

```
Match Address 192.0.2.8 User mwlucas
        PasswordAuthentication yes
```

Permitted Match Configurations

You cannot use Match statements to adjust all possible sshd configuration options. Check the current sshd manual page for the complete list of supported options.

Placing Match Statements

All configuration statements that follow a Match statement belong to that Match statement, until either the file ends or another Match statement appears. This means that Matches must appear at the end of `sshd_config`. Consider the following configuration.

```
...
X11Forwarding no
PasswordAuthentication no

...
Match Group wheel
    X11Forwarding yes
Match Address 192.0.2.0/29, 192.0.2.128/27
    PasswordAuthentication yes
```

The two Match statements override the defaults. When a user in the wheel group logs in, `sshd` sets the X11Forwarding option to yes for that user. When a user logs in from the IP addresses in the ranges **192.0.2.0/29** or **192.0.2.128/27**, the PasswordAuthentication option is set to yes. If a user in the wheel group logs in from a listed address, he gets both options.

We'll use Match statements throughout the rest of the book.

Root SSH Access

Sometimes, it seems that you need to allow users to SSH into the system as root. This is a colossally bad idea in almost all environments. When users must log in as a regular user and then change to root, the system logs record the user account, providing accountability. Logging in as root destroys that audit trail. It also encourages users to modify the root environment to suit their working habits. Server programs are frequently started by root, and those environment changes can make those services unstable or actively destroy data. Tools such as sudo and pfexec permit user accounts limited degrees of privilege. If you need root access to run your backup program, use sudo instead of logging in as root.

Certain environments, particularly large server farms, are designed so that logging in as root is not only possible but preferable. These environments require public key authentication and log the key used to authenticate each session. Sudo can be configured to authenticate via an SSH agent so that a user's password is never exposed to the server. Most readers of this book do not work in that environment.

It is possible to override the security precautions and make `sshd` permit a login directly as root. It's such a bad idea that I'd consider myself guilty of malpractice if I told you how to do it. Chapter 12 discusses some ways to use `sudo` to avoid this requirement. Logging in as root via SSH almost always means you're solving the wrong problem. Step back and look for other ways to accomplish your goal.

Chrooting Users

At times a user needs a command prompt or some specific program, but you don't want to let the user access files outside his home directory. A directory the user cannot escape is called a *chroot*. (A chroot is also useful for SFTP, as shown in Chapter 6, but that requires much less configuration.) OpenSSH supports chrooting users with the *ChrootDirectory* option.

```
ChrootDirectory none
```

By default, sshd does not chroot users.

Populating the Chroot

A chrooted user cannot access anything outside the chroot. Any chroot you create will not have device nodes, shells, or other programs unless you place them there. When your restricted user logs in, sshd will fail to find a shell or home directory and immediately disconnect them. At a minimum, you must set permissions on the chroot directory, create a home directory for the imprisoned user, create device nodes, and install a shell.

The chroot directory must be owned by root and not be writable by the restricted user, just as you would not permit an unprivileged user to write to the system's root directory. If the restricted user can write to the chroot directory, sshd will not let them log in.

A user's home directory (as shown in the system's `/etc/passwd`) is expected to be available inside the chroot. If user pkdick's home directory is listed as `/home/pkdick`, and he is chrooted into `/usr/prisonroot`, you must create the directory `/usr/prisonroot/home/pkdick`. This directory should be owned by the user, just like a regular home directory, and should contain any necessary dotfiles.

Create device nodes inside a dev directory inside the chroot. With a chroot directory of `/usr/prisonroot`, you would need `/usr/prisonroot/dev`. The method to create device nodes varies between operating systems. OpenBSD and many Linuxes use the shell script `/dev/MAKEDEV`, while FreeBSD and many commercial UNIX-like systems use a device file system. On most systems, the chroot will require the device nodes `/dev/urandom`, `/dev/null`, `/dev/stderr`, `/dev/stdin`, `/dev/stdout`, `/dev/tty`, and `/dev/zero`. Some operating systems might require additional device nodes.

Finally, users need a shell. Copy a statically-linked shell into the chroot's `/bin` directory (e.g., `/usr/prisonroot/bin`). Also copy static versions of any other programs the user needs. You could add dynamically linked programs, but then you must also copy any necessary libraries.

Note that your operating system might include tools to easily populate a chroot, such as jailkit (http://olivier.sessink.nl/jailkit/), or other methods to simplify chroot management. Check your operating system documentation.

Assigning Chroot Directories

To chroot users, specify the users' root directory as the ChrootDirectory.

```
ChrootDirectory /home/convict
```

This works for a single user, or if all SSH users have the same chroot directory, but `sshd` offers the %%, %h, and %u macros to assign individual home directories.

If your chroot directory path includes a literal %, use the %% macro. Here, we chroot into the directory `/home/disk%1/convict`.

```
ChrootDirectory /home/disk%%1/convict
```

The %h macro expands to the users' home directory as specified in `/etc/passwd`. This entry will lock users into their assigned home directory.

```
ChrootDirectory %h
```

The %u macro expands to the user's username. This lets you assign a group of users unique home directories in a shared chroot directory.

```
ChrootDirectory /usr/prisonroot/home/%u
```

Choosing Users to Chroot

Use a Match statement to selectively chroot users.

```
...
ChrootDirectory none
...
Match Group billing
    ChrootDirectory %h
```

If a majority of your users are chrooted, reverse the default and allow your systems administrator full access.

```
...
ChrootDirectory %h
...
Match Group wheel
    ChrootDirectory none
```

Debugging a Chroot

If your chrooted user cannot log in, run `sshd` in debugging mode in a terminal window (see "Debugging sshd" earlier this chapter). Log in as a chrooted user and watch `sshd`'s output. `sshd` will probably tell you the problem. Common issues include missing device nodes, incorrect directory permissions, or a missing shell.

Protecting the SSH Server

Any Internet server will have random stuff poking at it. Worms, script kiddies, and other assorted scum would really like to break into your computer. If nothing else, someone wants to run an IRC bot on it. How can you protect your SSH service?

Some people recommend changing the TCP port that `sshd` runs on. This is a perfect example of security through obscurity. Scanners constantly probe all open ports on all Internet-connected IP addresses, and they're pretty good at figuring out what service is actually running on which port. Changing ports might buy you a couple of minutes against a dedicated intruder, but no longer. Changing ports can reduce the amount of random noise in your logs, increasing your odds of noticing real problems. You're better off having your firewall restrict access to known-friendly IP addresses.

Similarly, some people suggest changing the `sshd` banner. You see the banner when you `telnet` to the SSH port. The banner usually identifies the type of server. All SSH servers differ slightly, and might require special client settings. SSH clients use the banner to detect any quirks needed for a reliable connection with a particular server. If you change the banner to report *SSH-2.0-Paranoid* instead of *SSH-2.0-OpenSSH_5.6*, you're depriving clients of information they need to connect reliably.

OpenSSH has built-in protection through *privilege separation*. Only a small section of `sshd` runs with root privileges. Most of the server runs as an unprivileged user. This means that if an intruder successfully breaks into the OpenSSH server, he can only do a limited amount of damage to your system. It's still really, really annoying, mind you, but not devastating.

As with all Internet-facing services, a simple way to limit risk to your SSH service is to reduce the number of IP addresses that can access it. OpenSSH respects TCP wrappers (`/etc/hosts.allow` and `/etc/hosts.deny`). If your server runs a firewall, use it instead. By only allowing authorized IP addresses on your network to access your SSH server, you block the vast majority of attackers.

The most effective way to protect your server, however, is to disable passwords and only allow logins via keys. We cover access via keys in Chapter 7.

We'll return to configuring `sshd` when we cover particular SSH features, but for now let's examine client-side behavior.

Chapter 4:
Verifying Server Keys

If you're paranoid, or if you've been a system administrator for longer than a week, you need to be sure that the server you're actually logging into is the server you think you're logging into. Server keys help verify a server's identity before you enter your username and password into the wrong machine.

Network connections over unencrypted protocols (such as telnet) are easy to divert to the wrong machine. An intruder who controls a publicly accessible device, such as a server, can make it spoof a different server's identity. Every user that logs on to the spoof server gives his username and password to the intruder. This is a classic network attack that is still widespread today; the protocols change, the applications change, but the underlying attack is identical.

When properly deployed and used, SSH-2 categorically eradicates these spoofing attacks. Even if an intruder can make one machine resemble another, even if he copies the login prompts and the Web site and the operating system version, the intruder cannot copy the target server's private key unless he already controls the server. Without the private key, the spoof server cannot decrypt anything sent using the server's public key. SSH server keys verify the server's identity.

Every SSH server has a unique public key, as discussed in Chapter 2. The first time an SSH client connects to an SSH server, it displays the server's public key fingerprint to the user. The user is expected to compare the fingerprint shown with the server's key fingerprint. If they match, the user tells their SSH client to cache the key and the connection continues. If the keys don't match, the user terminates the connection.

On all subsequent connection attempts to that server, the client compares its cached key to the key presented by the server. If the keys match, the connection continues. If the keys don't match, the client assumes that something has gone wrong. The client aborts the connection and notifies the user.

For SSH server keys to be useful, you must verify that the key shown in the client is the key offered by the server. A public key is several hundred characters long, however. Systems administrators can't realistically ask users to compare hundreds of characters to a list of known-good host keys; most brains automatically dismiss the task as impossible. (It's very possible, but it is tedious and annoying.) OpenSSH summarizes public keys with fingerprints.

Key Fingerprints

A *key fingerprint* is an (almost) human-readable summary of a public key. View a key's fingerprint with the `ssh-keygen` program. Use `-l` to print the fingerprint and `-f` to specify a key file.

```
# ssh-keygen -lf /etc/ssh/ssh_host_rsa_key.pub
2048 99:8c:de:5d:59:b9:af:e7:ce:c6:20:92:94:e1:ce:04 /etc/ssh/
ssh_host_rsa_key.pub (RSA)
```

This example displays the fingerprint of the server public key in the file */etc/ssh/ssh_host_rsa_key.pub*. The key is a 2048 bit RSA key, and the fingerprint itself is the long string beginning with 99:8c and ending with ce:04. Record the fingerprint, as well as the fingerprints for the files *ssh_host_dsa_key.pub* and *ssh_host_ecdsa_key.pub*. You and your users will need the fingerprints when first connecting to the server.

The simplest way to collect all the fingerprints is to copy the fingerprints to a file, as shown here.

```
# ssh-keygen -lf ssh_host_dsa_key.pub > $HOME/keys.txt
# ssh-keygen -lf ssh_host_ecdsa_key.pub >> $HOME/keys.txt
# ssh-keygen -lf ssh_host_rsa_key >> $HOME/keys.txt
```

Now get those key fingerprints to your users.

You can use `ssh-keyscan` to retrieve public key fingerprints from SSH servers, but you must still verify those fingerprints against the server's public key. By the time you do that, you might as well extract the public key fingerprint from the server itself.

Making Host Key Fingerprints Available

A user first connecting to an SSH server should compare the host key fingerprint that appears in their client to a known-good host key fingerprint. They will only do this if the comparison process is easy, however. The system administrator needs to make fingerprint comparisons simultaneously easy and secure. The easiest way is probably to display the key fingerprints on an encrypted Web site accessible only from within your company or site. When an employee needs SSH access to the server, give them a link to the fingerprint page with their login credentials. Do not distribute key fingerprints over insecure media, such as email or an unencrypted Web site.

Chapter 11 offers methods to automatically distribute keys and fingerprints. Deploying these methods will eliminate the need for users to manually verify keys, simultaneously increasing compliance and decreasing workload.

Host Keys and the OpenSSH Client

When you first connect to an SSH server with the OpenSSH client, you'll see a prompt asking you to verify the key.

```
# ssh envy
The authenticity of host 'envy (198.22.65.226)' can't be established.
ECDSA key fingerprint is 67:d4:4e:53:93:e6:c2:dd:e8:54:8b:e9:d8:ff:68:6d.
Are you sure you want to continue connecting (yes/no)?
```

This is your opportunity to verify that the OpenSSH server is actually the host you think it is. Get your list of keys and compare the ECDSA fingerprint in the list to the ECDSA key fingerprint shown in the client. If the key fingerprints match, type yes to cache the verified key and continue the connection. You'll get a message much like the following.

```
Warning: Permanently added 'envy,198.22.65.226' (ECDSA) to the list of known hosts.
```

The next time you connect to this host, OpenSSH will compare the host key in the cache to the host key on the server and, if they match, connect silently and securely.

If you type no OpenSSH immediately disconnects. Immediately notify your systems administrator and/or security team that the host key does not match.

Host Keys and the PuTTY client

The first time you connect to a server with PuTTY, you'll see a warning much like in Figure 4-1.

Compare the key fingerprint shown in the client to the key fingerprint in your list. As of this writing, PuTTY doesn't understand ECDSA keys, so it uses the RSA key instead. Compare the RSA key fingerprint offered by PuTTY to the known-good server RSA key fingerprint.

If the keys match and you want PuTTY to connect and cache the key for future reference, hit "Yes."

Figure 4-1:
PuTTY Key
Fingerprint

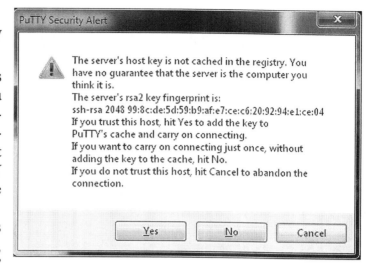

If the keys match, and you want to continue connecting but don't want PuTTY to cache the key, hit "No."

If the keys do not match, hit "Cancel." The connection will terminate. Immediately notify your systems administrator and/or security team of the non-matching host key.

Randomart Key Fingerprints

While verifying key fingerprints is much better than verifying the actual key, it's still annoying. The OpenSSH client and server support something easier than fingerprints, called *randomart*. A randomart image is a visual interpretation of a key fingerprint.

Unfortunately, the randomart algorithm is not yet finalized. You can experiment with this in the OpenSSH client and server, but don't assume that the randomart images will not change in different OpenSSH versions.

When Keys Don't Match

If a host key has changed, you'll get a message much like this:

```
$ ssh envy
@@@@@@@@@@@@@@@@@@@@@@@@@@@@@@@@@@@@@@@@@@@@@@@@@@@@@@@@@@@@@@@
@    WARNING: REMOTE HOST IDENTIFICATION HAS CHANGED!     @
@@@@@@@@@@@@@@@@@@@@@@@@@@@@@@@@@@@@@@@@@@@@@@@@@@@@@@@@@@@@@@@
IT IS POSSIBLE THAT SOMEONE IS DOING SOMETHING NASTY!
Someone could be eavesdropping on you right now (man-in-the-middle attack)!
It is also possible that a host key has just been changed.
The fingerprint for the RSA key sent by the remote host is
99:8c:de:5d:59:b9:af:e7:ce:c6:20:92:94:e1:ce:04.
Please contact your system administrator.
Add correct host key in /home/mwlucas/.ssh/known_hosts to get rid of this
message.
Offending RSA key in /home/mwlucas/.ssh/known_hosts:33
RSA host key for envy has changed and you have requested strict checking.
Host key verification failed.
```

Scary-looking stuff, no? It's supposed to be. Your SSH client is screaming that something is Very Wrong. If your desktop was an ambulance, the lights would be spinning and the siren blaring. The super-secret host key pair used to protect this system has changed. You must talk to the systems administrator and determine if:

⅄ The systems administrator destroyed the key pair (accidentally or deliberately) and generated a new one. He should have a new key fingerprint for you.

⅄ The fingerprint cached by your client is wrong. You might have a desktop security problem.

⅄ The server has been replaced or upgraded, and now supports a new key pair algorithm. The systems administrator should have a new key fingerprint for you.

⅄ The site uses round-robin DNS to have several servers share a single name, and you're connecting to the shared name rather than an individual server's unique name.

⅄ Your key cache is corrupt. You must re-validate this host key. Annoying, but not insurmountable. Your systems administrator can verify that the key has not changed.

⅄ An intruder controls the server, or has diverted your connection to a different server.

⅄ You, your systems administrator, and/or your security team are about to have a bad day.

When a key changes, immediately contact the system administrator. DO NOT CONNECT TO THE SYSTEM UNTIL YOU KNOW WHY THE KEY CHANGED. All of these are serious errors that require investigation.

If the key has changed for a legitimate reason, verify the new key. If the new key is correct, replace the old key with the new one. PuTTY will offer to replace the key for you, while in OpenSSH you must edit the key cache yourself, as discussed in Chapter 5. If the key is still not correct, talk to the systems administrator again. A legitimate SSH key change might mask an illegitimate intruder; I've seen more than one freshly-installed server get compromised before the first legitimate logon.

You can override an SSH client's refusal to connect to machines when their host key has changed, but remember, an SSH connection doesn't just validate the server and protect your data in transit. A completed connection also hands your authentication information to the SSH server. If you give your password to a compromised machine, you've just given the intruder your username and password. If you use the same password on multiple machines, you can no longer trust any of them. Cancel your weekend plans right now, and possibly next weekend's as well. You'll be busy recovering from backup and managing irate customers.

A mismatched public key means that OpenSSH works. Listen to it.

Chapter 5: SSH Clients

Client software resides on a user's personal machine and permits connections to an OpenSSH server. We'll cover two common clients: the OpenSSH command-line client for UNIX-like clients (ssh) and the freely available PuTTY client for Microsoft Windows clients. Both clients are freely usable and redistributable, in source or binary form, with very minimal restrictions, limitations, or license fees.

Purists will note that you can get an OpenSSH-based client for Windows systems, most easily through Cygwin. PuTTY has been ported to many Unix-like systems and mobile devices. These are less common, so I won't specifically cover them.

Each client has its own section in this chapter. Further chapters about SSH clients will be divided into three sections: one for the theory of what we're doing, followed by separate sections on configuring each client.

OpenSSH Client

The OpenSSH SSH client, ssh, is developed synchronously with the OpenSSH server. As new features often appear in OpenSSH before other SSH implementations, you'll get the bleeding edge of SSH features by using the OpenSSH client. The very newest OpenSSH client is available only in OpenBSD. Every so often, the OpenSSH software package is extracted from OpenBSD, modified to work on other operating systems, and released as OpenSSH-portable.

A user's personal SSH settings are recorded in files in the directory *$HOME/.ssh/*. This directory must be writable only by the user and root. Various client and server functions will stop working if others can write to this directory. (*$HOME/.ssh/* can be readable by other users.) While ssh creates this directory with correct permissions, verify the permissions if your SSH suite is behaving oddly.

To run ssh, enter the command followed by the host you want to connect to.

```
$ ssh envy.blackhelicopters.org
```

This uses your system's default settings to connect to the host **envy.
blackhelicopters.org**. (Specify your own hosts here; if you connect to this one, I might broadcast your username and password.)

Debugging SSH

If ssh isn't behaving the way you expect, try running it in verbose mode with -v. You'll see the server and client negotiate protocol version and encryption algorithms, the server present its host key, the client verify that key, and the two negotiate the various authentication methods. While this might not solve your problem, it will tell you where the login fails and give you a hint about where to look. Reading the output carefully might tell you that, for example, the server requires public key authentication for logons.

```
$ ssh -v envy.blackhelicopters.org
```

If you still have trouble, you can use multiple -v options to increase the amount of debugging.

SSH Configuration

Configure ssh's behavior by setting options on the command line or in a configuration file. Use configuration files for permanent changes and the command line for temporary changes. We'll consider the configuration file first.

Two files control SSH client behavior: */etc/ssh/ssh_config* and *$HOME/.ssh/config*. The former sets default SSH client behavior for all users on the system. The latter is the user's personal SSH client configuration. A user's configuration file overrides all global settings, but most users can't be bothered to enter their own custom configurations. Changes to the client configuration files affect all SSH connections started after the change. There's no process to restart, but changing your client configuration doesn't affect existing SSH sessions. Both files have the same syntax, and accept exactly the same options. I'll refer to *ssh_config* for brevity, but everything applies to *$HOME/.ssh/config* as well.

For example, certain worms search for SSH servers on TCP port 22 and try to guess legitimate user names and passwords for them. To avoid these scanners, you might run sshd on a port other than 22. If your site has this policy, tell your client to connect to a different port with the Port option.

```
Port 2222
```

With this entry in *ssh_config*, your client will use port 2222 for every outgoing SSH connection.

While most connection options can also be set on the command line, I recommend storing permanent information in *ssh_config*. Programs such as scp and sftp (see Chapter 6) read *ssh_config*, and the command-line options for each of these programs are slightly different. Using *ssh_config* gives you central cross-program configuration.

Per-Host Configuration

Change ssh's behavior when connecting to particular systems with the Host keyword. When I connect to any host in the **blackhelicopters.org** domain, my SSH client will attempt to connect to port 2222. All other hosts will be contacted on port 22, as specified in */etc/services*.

```
Host *.blackhelicopters.org
    Port 2222
```

I could also specify an IP address, or a network of IP addresses.

```
Host 192.0.2.*
    Port 2224
```

Note that ssh matches these *ssh_config* entries based on what the user enters on the command line. Host entries must be an exact case-insensitive match with what the user types.

Assume that my *ssh_config* file contains both Host entries above. First, I type

```
$ ssh avarice.blackhelicopters.org
```

This matches the first Host entry, so ssh connects to port 2222.

My desktop's */etc/resolv.conf* automatically appends the domain name blackhelicopters.org to any lone hostnames, so I probably wouldn't type my whole domain name. Instead, I'd just do something like this.

```
$ ssh avarice
```

This will not match my first Host entry, as I didn't explicitly type the domain name given in *ssh_config*. If the host **avarice** has an IP address in 192.0.2.0/24, though, wouldn't the second Host entry match? No, because the host entries match based on the command line; there is no check against DNS. To match based on the IP address in the Host entry, I would have to explicitly SSH to an IP address. Custom settings for this host require a Host entry like this.

```
Host avarice
    Port 2222
```

`ssh` parses conditions on a first-match basis. Configuration options listed after Host entries remain in effect until the next Host entry. This *ssh_config* is probably wrong.

```
Host *.blackhelicopters.org #WRONG
Host 192.0.2.*
    Port 2222
```

We have an entry for any host under the blackhelicopters.org domain, but there's no special configuration for it. Any hosts in 192.0.2.0/24 run SSH on port 2222. You probably wanted to use port 2222 for all hosts in blackhelicopters.org and all IP addresses in 192.0.2.0/24. Instead, list multiple hosts on the same line, separated by spaces.

```
Host 192.0.2.* blackhelicopters.org *.blackhelicopters.org
    Port 2222
```

I list both *.blackhelicopters.org and blackhelicopters.org because there is a specific machine named blackhelicopters.org. The leading asterisk and period before the domain name will not match that host. I could also add individual hostnames to the end of the list.

Put any defaults at the end of your config file. Servers not matched by previous Host entries will use those defaults.

```
Host 192.0.2.* blackhelicopters.org *.blackhelicopters.org
    Port 2222

Port 981
```

Here your default SSH port is 981, but the specified hosts use port 2222.

Alternate Configuration Files

To use a configuration file other than *ssh_config*, specify it on the command line with the `-F` option.

```
$ ssh -F $HOME/.ssh/test-config avarice
```

This lets you try changes and experiment with features without damaging your working configuration. Now that you understand how to use the `ssh_config` file, let's see some common options used in it.

Common SSH Options

The most common options people use when connecting via SSH are to change the username, the port, or add options.

Changing Usernames

The OpenSSH client (and most other SSH clients) assumes that your username is the same on both the local and remote systems and tries to log into remote systems with the same username you have on the local machine. On most of my computers, my username is **mwlucas**. Occasionally someone creates an account for me with a different username, such as **mlucas** or **lucas** or **michael** or **jerkface**. I must tell ssh to use a different username on the remote system. You do this by putting the user account name, followed by an @ symbol, then the remote machine name, as shown below.

```
$ ssh lucas@gluttony.blackhelicopters.org
```

You can also specify the username with -l.

```
$ ssh -l lucas gluttony.blackhelicopters.org
```

You can specify a different username in `ssh_config` with the User option.

```
Host gluttony.blackhelicopters.org
    User lucas
```

By storing usernames in the ssh configuration file, I can forget it and free up valuable brain space.

Changing Port

Some sites run SSH on a port other than 22, usually to provide an appearance of improved security. (It doesn't actually secure SSH, but people do it anyway, often just to reduce log noise.) Use -p and a port number to change the port your SSH client connects to. For example, if your SSH server runs on port 2222, connect with:

```
$ ssh -p 2222 gluttony.blackhelicopters.org
```

You can also specify a port in *ssh_config*.

```
Port 2222
```

Again, I recommend storing permanent connection information in *ssh_config*.

SSH Options on the Command Line

To use an option on the command line, use -o, an equal sign, and the desired option.

```
$ ssh -o Port=2222 blackhelicopters.org
```

This example is trivial — you would probably use -p to set a port instead typing out -o Port=2222. Some ssh options don't have a command-line flag, however, and -o lets you set them. The ssh manual page contains a complete list of options for all occasions.

You can use -o multiple times to set multiple options.

Multiplexing OpenSSH Connections

SSH sessions can take a long time to open, particularly if the SSH server can't find a reverse DNS entry for the client's IP address. Or you might have a firewall that limits the number of simultaneous TCP connections between network segments. Perhaps one of the machines is so old that the initial key exchange takes several seconds. OpenSSH supports connection multiplexing for these situations, permitting you to run several SSH sessions over one TCP connection. While this doesn't solve any of these problems for the initial connection, additional connections will start much more quickly. Multiplexing doesn't work well with X11 forwarding.

You must use the OpenSSH client and the OpenSSH server to support connection multiplexing, but no server-side configuration is required. Multiplexing does not work with PuTTY, nor with non-OpenSSH servers.

Configuring Multiplexing

The ssh client uses Unix sockets to manage multiplexed connections. The user must create a directory for these sockets, and set the permissions so that only he can read them.

```
# cd $HOME/.ssh
# mkdir sockets
# chmod 700 sockets/
```

Now enable multiplexing in *ssh_config*.

```
ControlMaster auto
ControlPath ~/.ssh/sockets/%r@%h:%p
```

The ControlMaster setting tells ssh to try to use connection multiplexing, but to fall back to a separate TCP connection should multiplexing fail. This lets you enable multiplexing as a default, but still connect to non-OpenSSH servers.

ControlPath tells ssh where to find the multiplexing management files. The %r macro expands to the username, %h to the host, and %p to the port. If I connect to the host avarice on port 2222 as the user **mwlucas**, ssh will automatically create the socket file *mwlucas@ avarice:2222* in the specified directory.

Risks of Multiplexing

Anyone who can read the multiplexing control files can access all data going over your SSH connections. Only use connection multiplexing on clients where you trust everyone who has root.

Copying a large file over a multiplexed SSH session can slow down your other sessions.

All of your SSH connections to a host actually run over the first connection opened to that host. If that connection dies, all child connections die with it.

Generally speaking, I recommend enabling multiplexing only on single-user desktop systems.

SSH Addressing Options

The OpenSSH client lets you choose how it uses TCP/IP, by setting the address family and the source address.

AddressFamily

Hosts can have both IPv4 and IPv6 addresses. AddressFamily tells the client to connect only over IPv4 (inet) or over IPv6 (inet6). The default is any, which means "connect over any protocol you can manage." Here we deliberately disable IPv6. as "inet" means only use IPv4.

```
AddressFamily inet
```

BindAddress

Computers with multiple IP addresses on a single interface default to originating all connections from the main IP address on that interface. This is not always desirable. For example, I have two different subnets routed to my house. My desktop's interface has an IP address in each subnet. One address is primary, the other is secondary. Some servers only accept connections from my desktop's secondary address.

More complicated machines might have multiple interfaces, each with a different IP address. In this case, the system will use the main IP of the interface closest to the destination server. That address might not be permitted to connect to a particular server.

In these situations, tell ssh to connect from an IP address other than the system's main address with the BindAddress option.

```
BindAddress 192.0.2.9
```

The Host Key Cache

The SSH client records approved host keys in *$HOME/.ssh/known_ hosts*. Each SSH server public key appears in *known_hosts*, much like this.

```
avarice,192.0.2.81 ssh-rsa AAAAB3NzaC1yc2...
```

Each line contains the machine's hostname and IP address, separated by a comma, then the type of key, then finally the public key itself. Each name you've used for the host appears on its own line. This example shows that I connected to this machine by typing ssh avarice. If I had run ssh avarice.blackhelicopters.org, the machine name would include the domain. If I used both the short and long names, the cache would contain two lines, each with identical key information and IP addresses but different host names.

You can manually combine multiple entries for one machine. Just add the additional names, separated by commas, to the beginning of the line.

```
avarice,192.0.2.81,avarice.blackhelicopters.org ssh-rsa AAAAB3NzaC1yc2...
```

Usually I don't bother with this. Extra lines in my known_hosts file don't disturb me. Others feel differently.

Updating the Key Cache

How do you want to update your key cache? In some environments, users must manually verify host keys and then manually add them to the key cache. In other environments, it's acceptable to automatically add new keys to the cache. Most commonly, users want ssh to ask them what to do. The StrictHostKeyChecking *ssh_config* option tells ssh how to treat new host keys.

If you want to only add host keys to *known_hosts* by hand, set StrictHostKeyChecking to yes. When you connect to a new host, ssh will present the host key and tell you to verify it and add it to known_ hosts yourself. You will not be able to connect until you add the key. Additionally, when a host key has changed, ssh will refuse to complete the connection, instead displaying a warning and telling you to verify the key. This is most useful when the systems administrator regularly updates */etc/ssh/known_hosts* (see Chapter 13).

```
StrictHostKeyChecking yes
```

At the other extreme, you can have ssh automatically add unknown host keys to *known_hosts*. By having your client accept all host keys, you have no opportunity to verify the host key. Accepting unverified host keys is dangerous, as discussed in Chapter 4. To blindly accept all host keys, set StrictHostKeyChecking to no. But don't do it.

By default, ssh displays unknown host keys and asks the user what it should do. You can either choose to accept the host key and have ssh add it to *known_hosts*, or reject the host key. StrictHostKeyChecking defaults to *ask*.

Choose the option that best suits your environment. Your home computer probably has different needs than a secure system run by the NSA or a criminal cartel.

Cache Security: hashing known_hosts

The *known_hosts* file contains a list of all the cached, verified host keys. If someone breaks into your desktop, they can use this as a list of SSH servers to target. As your SSH servers presumably share a common systems administrator, the technique used to penetrate your client might also work on any of the servers you log into. Additionally, systems administrators can override the permissions on your *$HOME/.ssh* directory and view the contents of *known_hosts*. The best way to prevent snooping is to change *known_hosts* so that it no longer contains a list of hostnames. This is accomplished by *hashing* the hostnames, just like passwords are hashed in */etc/passwd*. Computing original hostnames from the hash file is very, very difficult.

If you replace the hostnames with their hashes, nobody can read the host names from the file, nor can anybody compute hostnames from the file. When you connect to a host, however, ssh can easily compute the hash of the name of the host you're connecting to and use that for comparison.

A hashed *known_hosts* entry looks something like this:

```
|1|gpPFIk1I/Ai4aTETkcOd0...
```

To have ssh automatically hash new host keys it adds to known_ hosts, use the *ssh_config* option *HashKnownHosts*.

```
HashKnownHosts yes
```

This will not hash existing entries, however. Use ssh-keygen -H to hash your existing *known_hosts*.

```
$ ssh-keygen -H
/home/mwlucas/.ssh/known_hosts updated.
Original contents retained as /home/mwlucas/.ssh/known_hosts.old
WARNING: /home/mwlucas/.ssh/known_hosts.old contains unhashed entries
Delete this file to ensure privacy of hostnames
```

This command copies your existing *known_hosts* to *known_ hosts.old*, then hashes everything inside *known_hosts*. Verify that ssh can still connect to your usual hosts. Once you feel confident that your key cache is still usable, delete the unhashed known_hosts.old.

Note that some operating systems hash known_hosts by default. On those, you must set HashKnownHosts to no to get a plain-text known_ hosts file.

The PuTTY Client

PuTTY is a telnet, SSH, and serial client and terminal emulator for both Windows and Unix-like systems. It's available at http://www.chiark. greenend.org.uk/~sgtatham/putty/, or a Web search for "putty ssh" will take you straight there. While it's not written by the paranoiacs in the OpenSSH team, the freely-available PuTTY source code has been repeatedly audited and is probably the most widely deployed Windows SSH client software.

The PuTTY download page offers several downloads. I suggest you download the full installer that contains all the software. You won't need all of the included programs, but it'll be easier and faster than individually downloading the various programs. You can choose to just download PuTTY.exe if you prefer. PuTTY doesn't actually need an installer, as it will run from any location and without any special hooks into the operating system, but the installer creates shortcuts in the Start Menu and on the desktop and registers the programs with the operating system.

If you feel adventurous, you could download the PuTTY development snapshot instead. This includes all of the latest patches in PuTTY, but it might also contain newly-created bugs.

Start PuTTY and you'll get a screen like Figure 5-1:

Figure 5-1: PuTTY Startup Screen

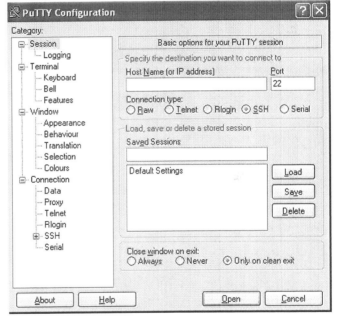

On the left side you configure options affecting how PuTTY presents itself and how it handles supported protocols. As you can see, PuTTY supports a variety of protocols. If you need a general-purpose terminal emulator, PuTTY can probably meet your needs. We're only going to cover SSH, however. Note the SSH option, second from the bottom. On the right side, you run SSH sessions.

If you select something on the left-hand side, the right side changes to show details on the selected option. Select SSH, and the right-hand side will show you a list of encryption ciphers, remote commands, and a whole bunch of protocol features that will only cause you trouble right now.

On a new PuTTY install I always set a default username. My accounts on my work systems all have the same username; the only time my username varies is when someone creates an account for me on their system, usually because they want me to do them a favor. I can set my username as a default in PuTTY, and thus never have to enter it when I start a session. Beneath the `Connection` box, I select `Data`. In the `auto-login username` space, I put my standard username.

Now I save this as my default settings.

Saving the PuTTY Defaults

To save new default settings, make your desired changes. Then select `Session` from the top of the left side. This will return you to the PuTTY main screen. Under `Saved Sessions` select `Default Settings`. Now select `Save`. When you open PuTTY, it automatically loads the settings you've saved here.

Note that changes to the default settings do not propagate to PuTTY sessions you've previously saved. If you change your defaults, and want those same changes to take place in a saved session, you must load, change, and save that session separately.

Starting SSH Sessions with PuTTY

In the main PuTTY screen, enter the hostname of your SSH server under `Host Name (or IP address)`. You can also change the port number here if necessary. Click `Open` at the bottom of the window. The PuTTY configuration window will disappear, replaced by a black terminal window.

Saving PuTTY Sessions

You can preconfigure PuTTY sessions, ensuring that your connections to a particular host happen the same way every time. Enter the SSH server hostname under `Host Name (or IP address)`. Under `Saved Sessions` type a name for this session. I usually name my sessions after the host, plus possibly a word or two for any special configuration in the session. I might have sessions labeled `dns1`, and another called `dns1 with X`, so that I can easily enable X11 forwarding when I need it.

To run a saved session double-click the saved name.

To copy a saved session, highlight it, click `Load`, make your changes, and save it under a different name.

PuTTY Management

You'll see a PuTTY icon in the upper left hand corner of your running PuTTY icon. This leads to a drop-down menu of useful tasks.

To duplicate an existing session, opening a second window to the same host, select `Duplicate Session`.

To open a new window to a host that you've already saved a configuration for, select `Saved Sessions` and the session name.

To open a window to completely new host, select `New Session`.

PuTTY Copy and Paste

PuTTY does not use the standard Windows cut-and-paste shortcuts. To copy text in a PuTTY window, just select it with the mouse. To paste text, click the third mouse button (or mouse buttons one and two simultaneously) or use `SHIFT-INSERT`.

PuTTY Configuration

PuTTY's configuration is kept in the Windows Registry, under *HKEY_CURRENT_USER\Software\SimonTatham*. To move your PuTTY configuration from one machine to another, copy this section of the registry to another computer. You can even use this to distribute valid PuTTY configurations to your users through Active Directory.

Debugging PuTTY

PuTTY has two debugging facilities: the Event Log and the session log.

The Event Log records what happens during the existing SSH session. You can see the name, IP address, and port you connect to, the server's key fingerprint, encryption algorithms selected, and all the various negotiations required to establish an SSH session. To view the Event Log, click the upper left corner of your PuTTY window and go down to Event Log.

For serious debugging, use a session log. Before opening your SSH session, go to the `Session → Logging` window. You can select several different types of log. I usually choose `All session output`. Give PuTTY a name and directory for the debugging file. This file will contain a large amount of detail about the SSH session, much like the OpenSSH client's debugging option.

Both PuTTY and OpenSSH's `ssh` provide a terminal session on an SSH server. Now let's see how to copy files over SSH.

Chapter 6:
Copying Files over SSH

While SSH provides secure connectivity for command-line connections, how about transferring files? FTP (File Transfer Protocol) was the standard for many years. FTP even predates TCP/IP, the protocol underlying the modern Internet. It has all of telnet's security problems. Other old protocols, such as RCP (Remote Copy), are even worse.

There are many ways to transfer files over SSH. Applications such as `rsync` can use SSH as a transport mechanism. Some window managers include SSH transfer tools. We'll cover two particular protocols, SCP and SFTP, for both Unix-like and Microsoft systems, but be aware that there are many other tools as well.

SCP, or the *secure copy* protocol, was designed as a replacement for RCP. SFTP, or *Secure FTP*, is a protocol to replace FTP. It's an interactive protocol, allowing you to browse remote file systems. OpenSSH includes the client programs `sftp` and `scp`, while Windows clients can use WinSCP for both SCP and SFTP.

File Copy with OpenSSH

OpenSSH includes two file transfer programs, `scp` and `sftp`. We'll start with the simpler but less flexible program.

scp

`scp` copies individual files. The syntax is very simple:

```
$ scp source-hostname:filename destination-hostname:filename
```

You'll be asked for a password on the remote machine, just as if you were logging in via `ssh`. Once you enter the correct password, `scp` transfers the file over an encrypted channel.

If you don't enter an element in the command, it's assumed to be unchanged. For example, to copy the local file *data.txt* to the server **sloth**, run:

```
$ scp data.txt sloth.blackhelicopters.org:
```

I don't enter a machine name in the source area, so it's assumed to be the local machine. I enter a remote hostname, but not a filename, so the filename doesn't change. My file `data.txt` is moved to my login directory on the remote machine and the name is retained.

If a destination file already exists, `scp` will silently overwrite it. If the account does not have the necessary privileges to overwrite the file, the copy will fail. The `scp` program assumes that if you told it to overwrite an existing file, you had a good reason to. For this reason I recommend not copying files while logged in as root.

You must use a colon after a hostname. When you skip the colon, `scp` assumes that the argument is a file name. Here I copy the file `data.txt` to the file **sloth.blackhelicopters.org** on the local machine, just because I forgot the colon.

```
$ scp data.txt sloth.blackhelicopters.org
```

If I want to change the file name on the remote side, I would do something like this.

```
$ scp data.txt sloth:stuff.txt
```

I can also reach across the network, grab a file from a remote machine, and pull it back to my local workstation.

```
$ scp sloth:data2.txt data2.txt
```

You can copy files to or from any location on the filesystem that permissions allow.

```
$ scp sloth:/tmp/data2.txt /var/tmp/data2.txt
```

To recursively copy a directory to another machine, use the arguments `-rp`.

```
$ scp -rp /home/mwlucas sloth.blackhelicopters.org:
```

The `scp` program deliberately borrows many command-line options from the `cp` program. If you have more complicated copying needs, check the documentation.

`scp` is largely built on twenty-year-old `rcp` code. This makes adding new features difficult. If you have complicated file-copying requirements, look at `sftp`.

sftp

The SSH File Transfer Protocol (SFTP) is more flexible than SCP. Where SCP only copies files, SFTP permits many different file operations such as renaming and removing files, listing directories, and so on. SFTP commands are almost identical to FTP commands to simplify transition. The OpenSSH SFTP client is `sftp`. Anyone familiar with FTP already knows how to use SFTP, but we'll go through the basics.

```
$ sftp pride
mwlucas@pride's password:
Connected to pride.
sftp>
```

Once you've logged in, entering a question mark or the word *help* will list all the commands supported by the SFTP server. While the commands are almost identical FTP commands, we'll cover the basics.

To copy a file from your local computer to the server, use *put* and the file name.

```
sftp> put data.txt
```

To copy a file from the server to your local computer, use *get* and the file name.

```
sftp> get data.txt
```

To change the name of a file on the server use *rename*, followed by the current file name, then the new name.

```
sftp> rename data.txt old-data.txt
```

To change directories on the server, use *cd* and the directory name.

```
sftp> cd backups
```

To change directories on your client, use *lcd* and the directory name.

```
sftp> lcd Downloads
```

To end your SFTP session, use either `quit` or `exit`.

Changing Usernames

With either `scp` or `sftp`, if you use a different account name on a remote machine, add the account name and an @ sign before the server name, just as you would when starting an SSH session.

```
$ scp data.txt michael@sloth:
```

Other Per-Host Configuration

The scp and sftp programs read and use *ssh_config*. The manual page lists many command-line arguments for each program, but these arguments are not necessarily consistent with ssh. For example, scp and sftp let you choose a different server port with -P, instead of the -p used by the ssh client. To avoid confusion, I recommend always setting options in *ssh_config* or *$HOME/.ssh/config*.

File Copy with WinSCP

WinSCP is a SCP and SFTP client for Microsoft systems. It switches transparently between protocols depending on what the server supports.

Get WinSCP from http://winscp.net. While there's no fee to use WinSCP in your home or business, its license places restrictions on re-distributing the program yourself. If you wish to include WinSCP in a product, read the license carefully.

WinSCP comes with a standard Windows installer. The defaults are fine for most users, and include convenient features such as adding Win-SCP to the right-click menu when you select a file. The installer also installs Pageant and puttygen, which we'll use in Chapter 7.

When you start WinSCP, you'll get the screen in Figure 6-1.

**Figure 6-1:
WinSCP
Startup**

The left side contains areas where you can configure different features of your Win-SCP session.

The right side contains the settings for that area. The

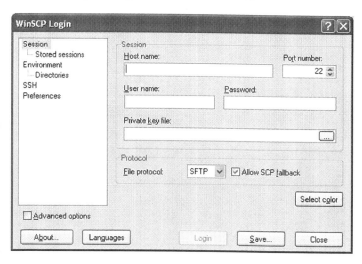

initial screen lets you configure a SFTP server connection, specifying a host name, username, and password. You can save this session for future use by clicking Save... and entering a name. WinSCP saves sessions named after the user and server name by default.

Setting WinSCP Defaults

Like PuTTY, WinSCP doesn't propagate changes through saved sessions. It's preferable to configure your default environment the way you want it before saving a bunch of SFTP sessions.

WinSCP accepts both SSHv1 and SSHv2 connections by default. You want to turn off SSHv1. Click SSH on the left-hand side, and set Preferred SSH protocol version to 2. Now click on Stored sessions and then Save defaults... You'll be prompted for confirmation. All WinSCP sessions you create from now on will default to only accepting SSHv2 connections.

Another useful WinSCP feature is the ability to import your PuTTY server key cache. On the Saved Sessions screen, select Tools->Import. You'll see PuTTY's key cache listed, with a check box by each. Make sure every server you want to use is checked, select Import cached host keys for checked sessions, and hit OK. WinSCP will now use your existing, verified key cache.

Using WinSCP

When you give WinSCP a correct username and password, it opens a double window. The left side shows your local home directory, while the right shows the remote server. This is called a "Commander-Style" interface. Drag and drop files from one side to the other.

You can also use the more common Windows-style interface, where WinSCP only shows the remote directory. To see a local directory, you must open a separate window. When creating your session, click on Preferences. Choose Explorer. Your WinSCP session will now look like a Windows desktop folder.

Configuring the SFTP Server

OpenSSH supports SCP and SFTP by default. There's very little to configure for either. For SCP, the scp program must be in the system's default $PATH. If the SSH server can't find scp, you'll get an error saying so. The `sshd` server is bundled with an SFTP server, activated by an entry in *sshd_config*:

```
Subsystem sftp /usr/libexec/sftp-server
```

The SFTP server requires no additional configuration.

SFTP-Only Users

You probably have some users that must copy files to a server, but don't actually need shell access. OpenSSH supports sftp-only users. This is most commonly combined with chroot (see Chapter 3), allowing the users to access to only a part of the filesystem. This is common with, for example, Web servers, where each individual customer only needs access to the files for their site. We'll cover that case.

I've created a system group called `sftponly`. By using a Match term in *sshd_config*, I deny these users access to anything beyond their home directory and only let them run SFTP.

```
Match Group sftponly
    ChrootDirectory %h
    ForceCommand internal-sftp
    AllowTcpForwarding no
```

That's it! No additional configuration is necessary.

Disabling SSH File Copy

You might want to disable the ability to copy files over SSH, while still letting users have command-line access. This is really, really hard. You can remove the `sftp-server` and `scp` commands from your server, and disable `sftp` in *sshd_config*, but that only disables the obvious ways to copy files. Users are tricky – especially frustrated users who think that the sysadmins are blocking them from doing what they need to do. They can copy files through any number of methods. Many of those methods will send unencrypted data across the network.

If you're really concerned about users copying files, I recommend using a chroot (see Chapter 3) and limiting what files they have access to.

Chapter 7: SSH Keys

An SSH public key identifies a server. SSH also supports authenticating users with keys. Using keys for user authentication is more complicated than using passwords, but when done correctly is far more secure. We'll consider both server and user keys.

Manually Creating Server Keys

If an intruder compromises your server, the server's private key is no longer private. You must replace it. This requires generating a new key pair. While most operating systems will automatically create a missing SSH key, others don't. Use `ssh-keygen` to manually create server keys.

If your server runs a recent OpenSSH version, run `ssh-keygen -A` as root to automatically generate all supported but missing host keys. This is a fairly new function, and might not yet be available on your system.

If your system is a little older, create the keys by hand.

```
# ssh-keygen -t rsa -f /etc/ssh/ssh_host_rsa_key -N ''
# ssh-keygen -t dsa -f /etc/ssh/ssh_host_dsa_key -N ''
# ssh-keygen -t ecdsa -f /etc/ssh/ssh_host_ecdsa_key -N ''
```

While any user can create SSH keys, only root can copy them to their final locations in */etc/ssh*. The -t flag specifies the type of key to create. Here we create three different types of keys: RSA, DSA, and ECDSA. The -f flag gives the filename of the public key file. The private key will be in the same location, with a .pub extension. If the ECDSA private key is in */etc/ssh/ssh_host_ecdsa_key*, the corresponding public key will be in */etc/ssh/ssh_host_ecdsa_key.pub*. Finally, -N lets you specify a passphrase on the command line. Server keys have no passphrase. The two single quotes indicate that the passphrase is empty.

Whenever you generate new server keys, be sure to get the key fingerprints as shown in Chapter 4. Your users will need the fingerprints to verify the fingerprints offered by the server.

Passphrases

What's this passphrase thing I just mentioned? A passphrase is like a password, but longer. It includes spaces, words, special characters, numbers, and anything else you can type. The passphrase is used to encrypt and decrypt the private key. A key with a passphrase cannot be used until someone enters the correct passphrase.

Passphrases are most often used with user authentication keys. A user with a key pair can access a system without providing a password for that system. Desktop and laptop systems are usually less secure than servers, and get infected, hijacked, or outright stolen depressingly often. If a user's authentication key pair is stolen, the intruder can use that key pair to access servers just as if he was the legitimate user! Encrypting the private key with a passphrase means that even if the users' private key file is stolen, the intruder cannot use the key without the passphrase. If an intruder gets either your private key file or your passphrase, but not the other, the damage is contained. Make the passphrase too long to guess by brute force and complex enough to discourage attempts to steal it.

Could a passphrase be a single word, like a password? Yes, but it's a *really* bad idea. Computers are now so fast that they can quickly discover short passwords rapidly by trying all possible passwords in succession. Using a short password for a passphrase considerably reduces your private key's security.

A passphrase should be at least several words long, something you can easily remember, and shouldn't be obvious to others – even to people who know you. Include special characters such as #, !, ~, and so on. Peculiar words from specialized non-computing vocabularies are useful. Substitute numbers for letters. Never use anything from pop culture, and never use any of your own personal catch phrases. Anything you've said to friends or co-workers that was catchy enough to repeat is a poor choice. If your imagination completely fails, Diceware (http://www.diceware.com) is a tool for randomly generating mostly-memorable passphrases from real words using ordinary dice. While intruders can ruin your week, a co-worker with your private key and a sense of humor can be even more aggravating.

Host keys do not use passphrases, because the SSH service must start when the system boots. You could use a passphrase with a server key, but SSH would not start until someone entered the passphrase at the server console. This is unacceptable in most environments.

User Keys

User key pairs provide stronger authentication than passwords. Combined with agents (see "SSH Agents" later this chapter), user keys eliminate the need to type any authentication information when logging into machines. Cryptographically, user keys are identical to host keys. The only difference is where the keys are used.

Speaking very generally, a computer identifies you based on something you are, something you know, or something you have. Iris scanners and fingerprint readers verify your physical body, something you *are*. A password verifies that you *know* a secret. Getting into a house requires that you *have* the door key. Key-based authentication combines two of these: you must *have* the file containing the private key and you must *know* the passphrase for that key. Admittedly, a private key file is easier for the owner to reproduce than a physical key – it's only copying a file – but it's more difficult to reproduce than an eight-character password. This additional layer of security provides extra protection against unauthorized use of an account.

Keys are more complicated than passwords, however. Just as you wouldn't leave your front door key hanging from the doorknob, you must protect your private keys. If the computer is lost or stolen, the key must be recovered from backup or it's lost forever. While it's possible to remember a password, most people won't put in the time or energy to remember the thousands of characters in a private key. (You do back up important documents on your workstation, don't you?) You also must prevent theft of your key. Just as you would change the locks if a thief had stolen your house key, you must be prepared to change your key pair if the private key is lost or stolen.

Risks of Passwords in SSH

For the last few years, a network of compromised machines dubbed the "Hail Mary Cloud" has scanned the Internet for SSH servers. When a member of this cloud finds an SSH server, it lets the other machines in the network know about it. The cloud then methodically tries possible usernames and passwords. One host on the network tries a few times, then another, then another. Blocking individual IP addresses is not a useful defense, because each address is used only a few times.

Any one attempt has low odds of guessing successfully. The attempts are constant. They never end. Eventually, the Hail Mary cloud will get lucky and break into your server. It might be tomorrow, or next year, but it *will* happen. To stop these types of attacks, you can either use packet filtering to block public access to your SSH server, or you can eliminate passwords on your servers. User keys let you eliminate passwords.

SSH Agents

Replacing a password with a passphrase and a private key has one obvious flaw: typing passwords is an annoyance. Why replace an annoying password with an even more annoying passphrase? It might be more secure, but are you really going to bother?

That's where an *SSH agent* comes in. An SSH agent is a small program that runs in the background. When you start a desktop session, you enter your passphrase to decrypt your private key. The decrypted private key is loaded into the SSH agent. The agent stores the key in memory, rather than on disk. When the SSH client needs the private key, it asks the agent to prove that the agent has it. The agent cryptographically signs the request with the decrypted private key. SSH accepts the signed request as evidence that the agent has the key. When you log off for the day, the SSH agent shuts down. The decrypted private key disappears from memory. In other words, with an SSH agent, you type your passphrase once per work session, no matter how many SSH sessions you open that day.

On a typical day I log into my workstation, activate my SSH agent, and type my passphrase once. I then open innumerable SSH sessions to servers and routers all over my network, without typing a passphrase or password again. When I log off for the day my agent shuts down. The memory used by the agent is wiped and returned to the operating system. My private key is once again only available as the encrypted file.

Agents do not guarantee security. Anyone who can read your computer's memory while you are logged in can access the decrypted key. This includes the root account. If you don't trust the system administrator on your desktop, don't use a private key. If you suspend your laptop, the decrypted private key remains in memory. Anyone who can wake your laptop can use the key as their access rights permit. A random thief interested in swapping your laptop for a quick buck probably won't know or understand what he has, but a thief who is specifically targeting you and/or your employer might check for a live SSH key. More commonly, if you don't lock your desktop before going to lunch, a coworker might play around with your systems. These problems are best solved by good computing practices.

Agent security is also a problem on multiuser machines. Anyone who has administrative or superuser privileges on your computer can access the SSH agent socket. If other people have root or Administrator access on your desktop, they can access your agent and masquerade as you. Using an agent might be unwise in this situation.

We will discuss SSH agents for both the OpenSSH and PuTTY clients later this chapter.

Installing Public Keys

No matter which client you use, you must install your public key on your server before you can log in with it. You haven't created a key pair yet, but you install keys from both clients in the same way.

When you log into a machine, the OpenSSH server checks the local file $HOME/.ssh/authorized_keys. This file contains public keys, one per (very long) line. The SSH server compares the public key offered by the client with the keys in the file. If the key matches, and the client can successfully exchange data with the key, then the client has demonstrated it has the users' private key. Access is granted. If there is no authorized_keys file, the server falls back to the next authentication method (usually passwords).

If you are a user requesting access to a server that only accepts public key authentication, the sysadmin will ask you for your authorized_keys file. Send him the public key file you would otherwise upload to the server. This is not a security risk – remember, your public key file is public. Anyone can have it. It's useless to anyone without the corresponding private key.

As of this writing, the most common type of user key is a RSA key. OpenSSH stores your RSA public key in the file $HOME/.ssh/id_rsa.pub. PuTTY's key generator lets you name your key files, but we'll assume you use the file name id_rsa.pub to make the examples easier.

To use your public key, you must copy it to the authorized_keys file in your account on the server. You can select and copy the public key in your graphic interface and paste it into the *$HOME/.ssh/ authorized_keys* file on your server, but this can introduce errors. Uploading the public key file via SFTP or SCP and then concatenating it onto *authorized_keys* is more reliable. Remember, each key must be on one and only one line in *authorized_keys*. More than one of my simple cut-and-paste attempts have turned to tears, then to threats of starting a new career as a llama smuggler, only to end in a manic-depressive binge at the nearest gelato shop. Have the machine copy the file. It's better at it than you.

Here, I copy my local *id_rsa.pub* to the SSH server sloth using scp. You could do the same thing with WinSCP's drag-and-drop features.

```
$ scp .ssh/id_rsa.pub sloth:
mwlucas@sloth's password:
id_rsa.pub 100% 418 0.4KB/s 00:00
```

The server will still request a password to upload the key file; even though you've created the key, it's not installed yet.

Now log into the server and append the contents of *id_rsa.pub* to the *authorized_keys* file. If this is the first time you're installing a public key, you could copy your public key to the *authorized_keys* file. If you get into that habit, however, one day you'll overwrite an existing *authorized_keys* and spend the next couple of hours kicking yourself for making such a simple mistake.

```
$ cat id_rsa.pub >> .ssh/authorized_keys
```

If another user can write to your *$HOME/.ssh* directory or to *authorized_keys*, he could add a rogue key to your account. The SSH server checks file permissions on the directory and the file. If other users can write to either, sshd realizes that the file is untrustworthy and ignores *authorized_keys*. Set your permissions appropriately.

```
$ chmod 600 $HOME/.ssh/authorized_keys
```

If key-based authentication doesn't work for you, check the permissions on *authorized_keys* and the *.ssh* directory.

If you're uploading from a UNIX-like workstation, you can do the upload and copy command in one action.

```
$ cat .ssh/id_rsa.pub | ssh server "cat >>~/.ssh/authorized_keys"
```

If you ever manually edit *authorized_keys*, be sure that each key ends with a newline. If your last entry doesn't end in a newline, the next key you add to this file will be tacked onto the end of the previous key. Both the new key and the old key will stop working. If in doubt, and you've edited the last key, hit RETURN at the end of the file before saving it. An extra newline at the end of *authorized_keys* won't hurt anything.

That's it! This machine will now accept logins to your account with your key pair.

Now let's see how to generate user keys with both OpenSSH and PuTTY clients.

OpenSSH User Keys

If you have a UNIX-like desktop, generate a key using the standard OpenSSH tools. Run ssh-keygen without any arguments, and the program will walk you through generating a key.

```
$ ssh-keygen
Generating public/private rsa key pair.
❶ Enter file in which to save the key (/home/mwlucas/.ssh/id_rsa):
❷ Enter passphrase (empty for no passphrase):
Enter same passphrase again:
Your identification has been saved in /home/mwlucas/.ssh/id_rsa.
Your public key has been saved in /home/mwlucas/.ssh/id_rsa.pub.
The key fingerprint is:
c7:f6:b2:f9:1b:c1:3a:c0:df:21:94:1d:e6:2b:21:29 mwlucas@avarice.blackhelicopters.org
The key's randomart image is:
+--[ RSA 2048]----+
…
```

You'll be asked ❶ where the new key should be saved. Always save SSH keys in the recommended locations, as the assorted OpenSSH software expects to find them there. The client asks for ❷ a passphrase, and to verify that passphrase. ssh-keygen encrypts your private key with this passphrase.

OpenSSH uses identical key formats for hosts and users. When you generate a user key, you get a key fingerprint and a randomart image. User key randomart isn't generally useful.

You'll find your new private key in *$HOME/.ssh/id_rsa* and your new public key in *$HOME/.ssh/id_rsa.pub*. Immediately back up your new key pair on offline media, such as a flash drive or CD-ROM. If you destroy your workstation, you'll want the ability able to recover your key pair.

Key Algorithms

Like host keys, user keys can use the RSA, DSA, or ECDSA encryption algorithms (see Chapter 2). If you don't specify an algorithm, the OpenSSH tools use the recommended algorithm – at this time, RSA. You can specify a different algorithm with the -t flag.

```
$ ssh-keygen -t ecdsa
```

Why create multiple keys? Cryptographers have this distressing habit of finding weaknesses in cryptographic algorithms. One day the unthinkable will happen and someone will discover a flaw in, say, the RSA algorithm, or OpenSSH's implementation thereof. All keys that use that algorithm will become untrustworthy. If you have user keys with different algorithms, you can disable the broken algorithm on your SSH server and still have server access.

Our examples will assume that you're using a RSA key, but they're just as applicable for DSA or ECDSA keys.

Using OpenSSH User Keys

First, install your public key in *authorized_keys* as described in "Installing Public Keys" earlier this chapter.

When your client finds a key pair in *$HOME/.ssh* and the SSH server finds an *authorized_keys* file in your account on that machine, the client asks you to enter your passphrase. Your client decrypts your private key and uses it to establish authentication with the server. Here I connect to the remote machine **sloth**:

```
$ ssh sloth
Enter passphrase for key '/home/mwlucas/.ssh/id_rsa':
```

Enter your passphrase, and you'll be logged in. Congratulations! Be sure that key-based authentication works before trying to implement an SSH agent.

Using the OpenSSH Agent

Any UNIX-like system with OpenSSH includes the SSH agent ssh-agent. With your key loaded into ssh-agent, your login attempts will look like this.

```
$ ssh sloth
Last login: Sun Aug 6 16:54:52 2011 from avarice
OpenBSD 4.9-beta (GENERIC.MP) #777: Tue Jan 18 13:56:34 MST 2012
$ uname -n
sloth.blackhelicopters.org
```

Note the absence of any request for a password or passphrase: you're just logged in to the remote machine. If you connect to a lot of machines during your working day, an SSH agent makes life much easier and transforms user keys from an annoyance to a pleasure.

One annoying thing about the multiplicity of desktop environments in the Unix-like world is that every environment has its own preferred way of running ssh-agent. We'll discuss a couple of them here, but if none of these work in your environment, you'll need to check the operating system documentation. Many operating systems have their own, slightly unique, desktop setups, and they change the precise method of adding keys to your SSH agent to suit the developers' personal prejudices.

Most X display managers, like xdm and kdm, have hooks to automatically check for SSH keys in the user's account. (A few operating systems, such as Ubuntu, require you create a symlink to tell the display manager to look for a key.) When the display manager finds a key during the logon process, it creates a pop-up window to request your passphrase. Enter your passphrase and the display manager will attach the SSH agent to your desktop environment. You're ready to begin work.

If you're more old-fashioned and run your desktop with startx, tell the SSH agent that you have keys with ssh-add before running startx.

```
$ ssh-add
Enter passphrase for /home/mwlucas/.ssh/id_rsa:
Identity added: /home/mwlucas/.ssh/id_rsa (/home/mwlucas/.ssh/id_rsa)
```

Enter your passphrase to enable your agent.

Text console users must first run ssh-agent with their shell as an argument, and then run ssh-add.

```
$ ssh-agent /bin/tcsh
$ ssh-add
```

All SSH sessions that start from this console session will run with the agent. If your console supports multiple virtual terminals (i.e., any BSD, Linux, etc), the SSH agent will only work for the process environment where you ran these commands. Another virtual terminal won't be able to access the agent; it will require its own SSH agent.

If you have multiple keys with the same passphrase, `ssh-add` auto-matically decrypts all of the keys. If the keys have different passphrases, `ssh-add` prompts you for each passphrase separately.

Using Nonstandard Key Files

OpenSSH programs automatically check for keys in the files *$HOME/.ssh/id_ecdsa*, *$HOME/.ssh/id_dsa*, and *$HOME/.ssh/id_rsa*. If you have a key file in a different location, you must explicitly inform the program about it. To use a particular key file with `scp`, `sftp`, or `ssh`, use the `-i` flag and the file path.

```
$ ssh -i $HOME/specialkey sloth
```

You'll be prompted for the key passphrase. To add a nonstandard key file to your SSH agent, give the file name to `ssh-add`.

```
$ ssh-add $HOME/specialkey
```

These keys are most often useful for automated processes (see Chapter 13).

We've only touched on the most frequently-used function for OpenSSH key management. For full details, read the manual pages for `ssh-keygen` and `ssh-add`.

PuTTY User Keys

Use the PuTTYgen program to create PuT-TY key pairs. PuTTY-gen is included in the PuTTY installation, or you can download it from the Web site. When you start PuT-TYgen, you'll get a screen like Figure 7-1.

Figure 7-1: PuTTY-gen Startup

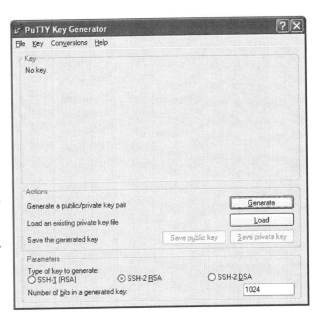

Verify that SSH-2 RSA is selected, and that the number of bits is not less than 1024. More is not necessarily helpful. (You might use fewer bits for keys dedicated for ancient servers, such as VAXes.) Click `Gen-erate`. The next PuTTYgen screen asks you to generate randomness by moving the mouse over the blank area. Once you generate sufficient entropy, PuTTYgen creates your key. The next screen displays the key information.

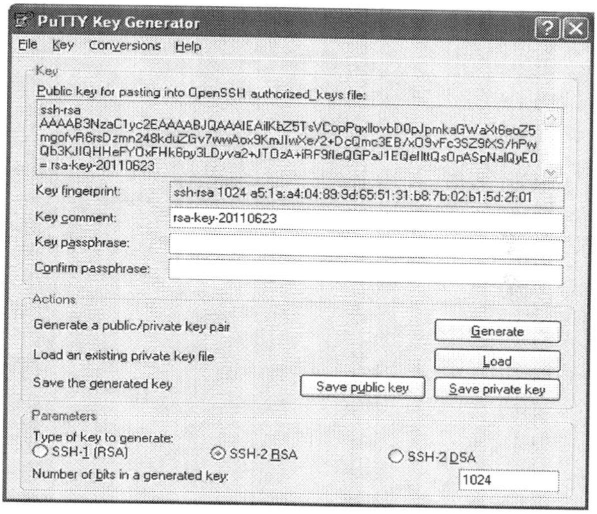

Figure 7-2: PuTTY-gen Passphrase

Enter your pass-phrase twice. If you want, you can add a comment. The default comment is the type of key and the date, but some people suggest using your email ad-dress or some other de-tail that differentiates between keys.

Then click `Save public key`. You'll get a standard Windows `save as` dialog box asking you to choose a location to save the key file. Save the file in a lo-cation that only you have permissions to access. You can use a folder under My Documents, but make sure you go in later and set the permis-sions so that other users on your machine cannot view the file. Save the file with a `.pub` extension.

Now save the private key. I strongly recommend using the same file name for the public and private keys. PuTTYgen uses a .ppk extension for private keys, so they won't overwrite each other. For example, the key files I use in my day job are named *mwlucas-work-20101114.pub* and *mwlucas-work-20101114.ppk*.

You now have a public key. Congratulations!

The key is stored in a format used by Pageant and PuTTY. This is different than the format used by the OpenSSH server. PuTTYgen can export the public key in a couple different formats, including OpenSSH.

Select `Conversions → Export OpenSSH Key`. You'll get a standard Windows dialog box asking you to choose a filename. That file is your OpenSSH-friendly public key.

Using PuTTY User Keys

First, install your public key in `authorized_keys` as described in "Installing Public Keys" earlier this chapter. Remember, use the exported OpenSSH-friendly version of the key, not the PuTTY-friendly version.

I strongly recommend using the PuTTY agent for normal use. You don't want to diagnose key and agent problems simultaneously, however. Make one connection without the agent to verify that your public key is properly installed on your server.

If you don't have an agent running, you must tell PuTTY where to find the private key file. On the left side of the PuTTY Configuration screen, select `Connection → SSH → Auth`. In the text box labeled `Private key file for authentication:`, put the full path to the private key. Remember, the private key file ends in `.ppk`. Now try to connect. PuTTY will prompt you for your username and then request the private key passphrase. If you enter the passphrase correctly, you'll get a command prompt. If not, you won't.

Do not save this test connection. If you list a key file in your saved connection, PuTTY will bypass the agent every time you try to log in.

Once you know that your key works, reduce how often you must type your passphrase with the Pageant SSH agent.

Using the PuTTY SSH Agent

The PuTTY SSH agent, Pageant, stores your decrypted private key in memory and provides an interface for PuTTY to access it. You type your passphrase into Pageant only once. Every time you open an SSH session, PuTTY asks Pageant for proof that it has the private key.

Start Pageant by double-clicking on it. Ideally, you'd add a Pageant shortcut to the Startup folder, so that Windows starts Pageant every time you log in. The Pageant icon, a computer with a black broad-brimmed hat, will appear in the system tray.

Right-click on the Pageant icon. You'll see several options, including `View Keys`, `Add Key`, and `Exit`. There are also options for running a saved or new PuTTY session. Select `Add Key` to bring up a standard

Window file browser. Find your private key file and select it. Pageant will display a dialog box to request your passphrase. Enter it. If you enter your passphrase incorrectly, Pageant will ask again.

Once you enter your passphrase, Pageant is ready. Open up a PuTTY session. Connect to a machine that has your private key installed. You should get a command prompt without needing to enter a password.

If key-based authentication works when you specify a private key file, but not when using Pageant, be sure that PuTTY is configured to use Pageant. PuTTY uses Pageant by default but to verify it, on the left side of the PuTTY Configuration screen, select Connection → SSH → Auth. Under Authentication Methods you'll find an Attempt authentication using Pageant checkbox. Be sure it's checked.

Backing Up Key Files

If you lose your private key, your key pair is useless. Once you know your key pair works, back up both the private and public keys. The PuTTY .ppk file contains both the public and private keys, but the OpenSSH keypairs need both files. Don't just copy your private key to another machine – every machine that has your private key is another place your key can be stolen from. Back up your private key on offline media, such as a flash drive or a CD. You might also encrypt it with a program such as GPG. (If you're not familiar with GPG I recommend the book *PGP & GPG: Email for the Practical Paranoid*, by yours truly.)

Keys and Multiple Machines

Many systems administrators have multiple computers. I regularly use two desktops and a laptop. It is possible to move key pairs between machines just by copying the key files. You can even import OpenSSH keys into PuTTY. How do you realistically manage a single key between multiple machines?

Don't.

Rather than copying a single private key between multiple desktops, create a separate private key for each. When a particular machine is decommissioned, stolen, or self-immolated, remove the corresponding public key from the authorized_keys file on your servers.

If one of your desktops is compromised, you must remove that machine's public key from the authorized_keys file on your server. If all of your clients share a single private key, you must regenerate a new key pair and distribute it to all of your machines. The intruder who has your private key might well lock you out of your own systems before you can accomplish this. If each machine has a separate key pair – even if they all share the same passphrase – then compromise or loss of one key does not compromise the keys on all your other machines.

Also, preferred key algorithms change over time. As I write this, the recommended user authentication key is RSA, but I would not be surprised to see ECDSA become preferable in another year or two. By creating a new key whenever you get a new machine, and invalidating keys associated with old hardware, you ensure that your keys are relatively recent and secure.

Disabling Passwords in the SSH Server

Passwords are less secure than keys. Now that you have working authentication keys, the smart thing to do is to disallow password-based authentication. The `sshd_config` option *ChallengeResponseAuthentication* enables or disables generic challenge-response authentication systems, such as prompts requesting a username and a password. The option *PasswordAuthentication* enables or disables passwords. To disable password authentication, set both of these options to no.

```
ChallengeResponseAuthentication no
PasswordAuthentication no
```

While `sshd` permits public key authentication by default, verify that nobody's changed that. The PubkeyAuthentication option must be yes for key authentication to work.

```
PubkeyAuthentication yes
```

Now restart `sshd`, either with the built-in system command or `pkill -1 sshd`.

Changing `sshd_config` will not change how other programs use passwords. If you use passwords in `sudo`, `sudo` will still ask the user for their password.

Password Authentication Warning!

If you make a mistake in configuring SSH such that nobody can log in, you can lock yourself out of your server. Do not log out of your existing SSH session. Create a new SSH session. Verify you can log in and become root before disconnecting your first session.

The preceding paragraph is very important. Ignore it at your peril, or be prepared for your own manic-depressive gelato binge.

Permitting Passwords from Select Hosts

Perhaps you cannot completely disable passwords. You might have a few users or applications that cannot use keys for one daft reason or another. You must fix those reasons, but while you're working on that, you can allow passwords from specific hosts with conditional configuration, as discussed in Chapter 3. Here, we allow password authentication from a particular subnet.

```
Match Address 192.0.2.0/24
    PasswordAuthentication yes
```

Remember, all Match statements go at the bottom of your configuration file.

It is possible but extremely unwise to permit password authentication based on username. The SSH server must prompt a user to enter a username before rejecting the connection, rather than hanging up on clients that request passwords. This means that the Hail Mary cloud will continuously poke at the server. The account that permits passwords will be a weak spot. The reasons that compel you to permit limited password authentication probably make requiring a strong password just as difficult.

Agent Forwarding

Suppose I've disabled password-based authentication on all of my computers. The only way to access a command prompt on any of my computers is through using public keys. I'm working on my server **wrath. blackhelicopters.org**, and must copy a file over to **gluttony. blackhelicopters.org**. This presents a problem. My private key isn't on wrath. Copying the private key to a server is poor security practice – you want your private key on as few machines as possible. But password authentication doesn't work. How can I use `scp` or `sftp`?

The answer is to forward authentication requests back to your workstation for processing. Agent forwarding creates a socket on the SSH server, in a location shown by the environment variable $SSH_AUTH_SOCK.

```
$ echo $SSH_AUTH_SOCK
/tmp/ssh-DgE03f0MdJ/agent.92532
```

When you try to SSH from one SSH server to another SSH server, your SSH client on the server routes private key requests through this socket and back to your desktop.

To use agent forwarding, both the client and the server must permit it and the SSH agent must be running before starting your first SSH connection.

Agent Forwarding Security

The risk of agent forwarding is that you must trust the remote system. Anyone who has root can access the SSH agent socket, as can anyone who has the necessary privileges. Anyone who can access the SSH agent socket can use your private key without providing a passphrase.

If the remote server is compromised, the intruder can piggyback onto your authentication socket to log into remote servers with your credentials. While proper `sudo` permissions should limit the damage the intruder inflicts, this is still bad. Promiscuous agent forwarding has been responsible for intrusions in many organizations, even organizations you think would know better. Only enable agent forwarding to machines that you control.

Agent Forwarding in sshd

To enable agent forwarding in `sshd`, check this option in *sshd_config*.

```
AllowAgentForwarding yes
```

I'll frequently disable agent forwarding globally, then use a Match statement to permit only certain usernames or addresses to forward their agents.

OpenSSH Client Agent Forwarding

In *ssh_config*, use the ForwardAgent option to activate agent forwarding.

```
ForwardAgent yes
```

If both client and server support and permit forwarding, authentication requests will be forwarded.

PuTTY Agent Forwarding

PuTTY enables agent forwarding by default. On the left side of your PuTTY session, go to `Connection → Data → SSH → Auth`. Under

`Authentication Parameters`, you'll see a checkbox labeled `Allow agent forwarding`.

If both client and server support and permit forwarding, authentication requests will be forwarded.

You can use key authentication and `authorized_keys` to very specifically restrict what a user can do over SSH. We'll look at that in Chapter 12. Now, let's look at forwarding X11.

Chapter 8:
X11 Forwarding

Unix-like systems use the X11 (or just X) protocol for a graphic user interface. X has improved over the years, but it's still famously baroque. One of X's more useful features is the separation between the computer the program runs on and the display. You can run a program on one system, and have the display appear on another workstation. I can run my Web browser on my server on the public Internet and display the browser's interface on my laptop inside my employer's firewall, bypassing the firewall's content filter restrictions (for legitimate work reasons, of course). In this scenario all Web requests originate from my server, and the results would appear on my laptop.

Similarly, one of my favorite application debugging tools is the Wireshark packet sniffer. If you're not familiar with Wireshark, get a copy of Chris Sanders' *Practical Packet Analysis* (No Starch Press, 2007). If I have a problem with NFS, Apache, or any other network application or protocol on a remote server, I'll forward X from the server to my workstation and start sniffing packets on the server. The display shows up on my workstation.

If you've never used X before, the idea might seem a little strange. That's okay. Play with it and you'll quickly understand its usefulness.

Vanilla X transmits information across the network, but it's unencrypted, insecure, and uncompressed. Secure X data in transit by wrapping it inside SSH through *X11 forwarding*.

X11 Security

The original X protocols were not designed for security, and retrofitting security into any protocol isn't as effective as we would hope. Displaying X from a remote machine requires trusting the remote machine. The more you trust the remote machine, the more X programs you can run on that machine and display locally. If you fully trust a compromised machine, the intruder can use X to take over your workstation, capture your keystrokes, and access your systems as if he was you.

Only permit X11 forwarding to users or hosts that actually need X access.

The X Server

The X server runs the graphic display. The X client runs the software. The X server is probably your desktop – that's where the program's graphic interface appears. Your system must have an X server to use X11 forwarding.

Almost all Unix-like systems include an X server, usually from X.org but perhaps a vendor's proprietary system. If you're running Windows, you'll need a third party X server. I'll cover that when discussing PuTTY and X11 forwarding.

X11 Forwarding on the SSH Server

To enable X11 forwarding, make this entry in *sshd_config*.

```
X11Forwarding yes
```

Restart (or `pkill -1`) `sshd` after making this change.

The server must have a working `xauth` program to support X11 forwarding.

The manual mentions several other options for setting the fine details of X11 forwarding, but the overwhelming majority of readers will never need any of them. If you have an odd problem, though, check the various X11 options in the *sshd_config* man page.

X11 Forwarding in the OpenSSH Client

The OpenSSH client supports two levels of X11 forwarding, differentiated by desired security level. Configure both in *ssh_config*.

Basic X11 forwarding supports only a less-insecure subset of the X11 protocol. This level of X11 forwarding is fairly safe. Intruders cannot, say, take over your desktop or snoop your keystrokes with this level of X11 forwarding.

```
ForwardX11 yes
```

Always try this basic X11 forwarding first.

Many programs use X functions other than the secure subset. When forwarded over SSH, these programs show an error and crash. You can choose to allow the full set of X functions with the option ForwardX11Trusted.

```
ForwardX11Trusted yes
```

Trusting X11 permits all X functions. An intruder on the SSH server can capture everything on your local screen and your every keystroke. Be really, really sure you trust every single remote server you might ever log into before permitting this level of trust globally. And once you're absolutely certain – don't do it.

Per-Host X11 Forwarding

You can configure per-host settings to restrict X11 forwarding to only necessary hosts. I have a program on **pride.blackhelicopters.org** that requires fully trusting X11, so I make a special entry in *ssh_config*.

```
ForwardX11 no
Host pride.blackhelicopters.org
    ForwardX11 yes
    ForwardX11Trusted yes
```

Now I only have to worry about X software on one host, not every host I might SSH into.

Forwarding X on the Command Line

Even better than restricting X forwarding to certain hosts is enabling it on a connection-by-connection basis. In the previous example I enabled ForwardX11Trusted for all connections to the host **pride.blackhe-licopters.org**. I have a program on that host that needs full X access, but I don't run that program every time I log in. You can activate standard X forwarding when necessary with the -x command-line option.

```
$ ssh -X pride.blackhelicopters.org
```

If you must fully trust the remote host, equivalent to ForwardX11-Trusted, use -Y.

```
$ ssh -Y pride.blackhelicopters.org
```

This eliminates the risks of routinely forwarding X, but supports X forwarding when necessary.

X11 Forwarding with PuTTY

The first problem with forwarding X11 to a Windows desktop is that Windows does not include a X server. Windows cannot display X clients without additional software. Several companies offer Windows X servers, such as LabF, NetSarang, MKS, and MicroImages. There are also several free options, such as Cygwin. Use any X server you like. While this book covers Xming, the principles apply to all X servers, so don't worry if your employer or coworkers insist you use a different one.

Xming

Xming is a widely used and frequently updated X server for Microsoft systems. The most recent version of Xming is only available to people who donate to the project, but an older version is free. As with all of the software in this book, if you find Xming useful, I encourage you to donate to the programmer. Xming brings to Windows all sorts of X tricks familiar to Unix-like users, but for our purposes we'll just use it to display programs running on a remote server.

Download Xming from http://sourceforge.net/projects/xming/. The Xming installer is very straightforward to any Windows user, so I'm not going to walk you through it. Take the defaults. Once you complete the install, run Xming to start the server.

Enabling and Disabling X Forwarding

PuTTY forwards X by default. What's more, PuTTY does no security-based filtering of X11; its forwarding is equivalent to the OpenSSH client's ForwardX11Trusted. For this reason, I recommend disabling X forwarding by default, then enabling it only as needed.

On the left-hand side of the PuTTY Configuration screen, select Connection → SSH → X11. The first check box is Enable X11 Forwarding. Deselect it, then save the Default Settings. Leave the other settings unchanged, as they're only useful in uncommon situations.

Is Forwarding Working?

Your SSH session won't look any different after you forward X. How can you prove this is working before you need it?

If SSH has successfully negotiated X11 forwarding, it will set the $DISPLAY variable in your shell.

```
server$ echo $DISPLAY
localhost:10.0
```

Your shell knows that there's a X server attached to it. You can use your X program.

If it just isn't working, $DISPLAY is undefined. Below, X11 for-
warding is not working.

```
server$ echo $DISPLAY
$
```

If you get Undefined variable or something similar, SSH did not
successfully negotiate X forwarding. Check your system log, or the debugging log of your SSH client.

A connection using XDMCP will have a $DISPLAY value some-
thing like remote:1. Do not use it; instead, figure out why forwarding
over SSH is not working.

Do not run your X programs if $DISPLAY looks wrong!

Now run an X program from that terminal. It should display on
your desktop. Most X clients include the xterm terminal emulator. Run
xterm in the background on the SSH server.

```
$ xterm &
```

You'll get a command prompt back on the SSH server. In a moment
or two, depending on the bandwidth and latency between your server and
client, a terminal on the remote system will appear on your desktop.

If you don't like xterm, try xclock, xeyes, or xcalc instead.

When you connect with X11 forwarding enabled, you might see a
warning such as untrusted X11 forwarding setup failed or No
xauth data. These warnings are not critical when forwarding X over
SSH, and should not worry you.

Remote X Commands with OpenSSH

Logging into another machine just to run an X program can be an annoyance. The -f option for ssh tells the client to background itself just
before running the command. For example, if I want to run Firefox on
wrath.blackhelicopters.org, I could run:

```
$ ssh -f wrath firefox
```

The client will connect to the remote machine and display whatever
login text the remote machine shows. The ssh client then goes into the
background, restoring your command prompt on your local system even
as it runs the command on the remote system.

Note that remote commands are run in the users' full login environment. Any files attached to the users' shell, such as .cshrc or .profile,

are sourced. This might give you trouble, depending on the application you're running.

Backgrounding forwarded X-over-SSH sessions is very useful for particular situations, but forwarding TCP ports over SSH is even more useful. We'll look at that next.

Chapter 9: Port Forwarding

Port forwarding over SSH is a divisive topic.

SSH can serve as a wrapper around arbitrary TCP traffic. You can cloak unencrypted services such as telnet, POP3, IMAP, or HTTP inside SSH, securely transporting these insecure protocols. An SSH session can carry any TCP/IP protocol, including protocols your local IT security team has forbidden on your network. For this reason, many organizations with high security requirements do not allow SSH to cross their network. Organizations that have less stringent requirements use this ability to secure their enterprise. (You can also use SSH to create a VPN to carry all IP protocols, but that's in Chapter 13.)

For example, I manage my Web site and blog with WordPress. It provides a friendly pointy-clicky interface for web site administration, giving me a nice-looking site without actually needing to learn anything about Web design. My HTML education ended about 1996, and I have no desire to resume it. Traffic to and from my Web site is unencrypted, but I don't want to transmit my administrative username and password over the Internet in clear text. I use SSH port forwarding to tunnel HTTP between my Web server and my desktop. This protects my credentials in transit and eliminates the risk of my password being stolen on the wire. This is a sensible and legitimate use of SSH port forwarding.

Suppose my desktop is inside a high-security network, however. The firewall tightly restricts Web browsing and blocks all file transfers. If I can use SSH to connect to a server outside the network, I could forward my desktop's traffic to that outside server to get unrestricted access to the Internet. I could upload confidential documents over SSH, and the firewall logs would show only that I made an SSH connection.

Tunnels versus Security Policy

If you're an organization's security officer, port forwarding might make you consider entirely blocking SSH. I understand. I've had your job. You should also know that a recalcitrant user can tunnel SSH *inside* DNS, HTTP, or almost any other service or protocol. The only way to absolutely block SSH is to deny all TCP or UDP connections from the inside of your network to the outside world, use a Web proxy that intelligently inspects traffic, and not allow your clients access to public DNS even through a proxy. I've seen one firm actually implement this type of security perimeter, and they had many many gaps and exceptions for particularly clunky business-critical software. If you cannot implement this in your environment but have stringent security requirements, you must work with your users to meet your security needs. I strongly recommend you establish a solid network traffic awareness program as well as some intrusion and extrusion detection, so you know when your network traffic deviates from the norm. Network administrators should read Richard Bejtlich's books on intrusion and extrusion analysis, as well as my own Network Flow Analysis, and implement the tools discussed.

As a user, the ability to tunnel arbitrary traffic over SSH does not mean you should. If your organization's security policy forbids port forwarding or tunneling, don't do it. If the policy says "use the Web proxy and stay off IRC," then listen. I am not responsible if you use these techniques and are reprimanded, terminated, or exterminated. (Even if we IT security officers are all petty tinpot despots who don't understand your very personal and deeply urgent *need* for IRC and Google+.)

Example Environment

For all of these port forwarding examples, I assume that the SSH client is behind a firewall. This might be anything from a corporate firewall to a home router. There are several other machines behind this firewall, including Web and email servers. The client is inaccessible to the public Internet; the outside world cannot connect to it.

The SSH server is on the public Internet. Anyone can connect to it, and it can freely access the rest of the Internet.

Types of Port Forwarding

The three types of port forwarding are local port forwarding, remote port forwarding, and dynamic port forwarding.

Local port forwarding redirects one port on the client to one port on the server. Essentially you're saying, "Grab such-and-such port on the SSH server and make it local to my client." Suppose you want to download your email from a server that only offers unencrypted POP3, but you have SSH access to the server. You can forward, say, port 2110 on your local machine to port 110 on your POP3 server. Configure your desktop to collect email via POP3 from port 2110 on the localhost address. SSH intercepts the request to port 2110 and patches it through to the mail server's port 110. Figure 9-1 illustrates the data flow of local port forwarding.

Figure 9-1: Local Port Forwarding Data Flow

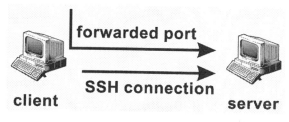

Remote port forwarding works in reverse. A port on the SSH server is forwarded to a port on your SSH client. You're saying, "Take such-and-such port on my client and attach it to the remote server." For example, suppose you have a workstation behind a firewall. You SSH from the workstation to a server on the public Internet. You could bind port 2222 on your public Internet server to forward traffic to your client workstation's SSH port. Anyone who connected to port 2222 on your public server would actually connect to the SSH server on your client. They could get inside the firewall without any other VPN client and without any regard for firewall rules. Figure 9-2 illustrates remote port forwarding.

Figure 9-2: Remote Port Forwarding Data Flow

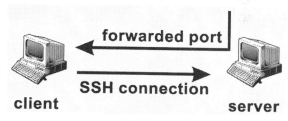

Dynamic port forwarding is a broader system, where many different client programs can connect to many different services. It creates a SOCKS proxy on the SSH client, and tunnels inbound requests to the SSH server. A SOCKS proxy is a generic gateway that can carry any TCP/IP traffic. (SOCKS doesn't actually stand for anything, by the way.) This would give anyone who connected to your client complete access to the network near the server. Figure 9-3 illustrates dynamic port forwarding.

Figure 9-3: Dynamic Port Forwarding Data Flow

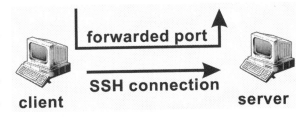

When the underlying SSH session dies, port forwarding stops. **Chapter 10** offers suggestions for keeping SSH sessions alive.

With these possibilities, it's easy to see why network administrators love SSH, and why many corporate environments forbid SSH.

Privileged Ports and Forwarding

On Unix-like systems, TCP ports below 1024 are reserved for system use. Only root can bind to those ports. As an unprivileged user, you can attach the local end of your SSH port forwarder to any port above 1024. You must use SSH as root to attach to a reserved port. Performing routine tasks as root is poor practice, so don't do it without really good reason.

Microsoft systems do not implement privileged ports. Anyone can bind to any open port on the system. The absence of port restrictions creates all sorts of amusing security issues, but it does make forwarding low-numbered ports no more difficult than forwarding any other port.

Local Port Forwarding

Before setting up local port forwarding, verify that normal SSH works. Determine the port on the server you want to forward to. Some typical choices are 80 (HTTP), 25 (SMTP), and 110 (POP3). All of these services are not usually encrypted on these ports.

Now choose a local port you want to use. Some clients work well when run on any port. You can generally configure an email client to check POP3 on any TCP port. Others don't. Web sites might choke if you change the port number. If you don't know how the protocol behaves when forwarded from one port to another, try it and see.

For our PuTTY and OpenSSH examples, I'm going to forward port 80 on my client to port 80 on the server, using the localhost address. Why? My Web site uses a Web-based content management system. While I could use a self-signed certificate to run HTTPS, I find port forwarding easier. I add an entry in my client's hosts file (either */etc/hosts or*

C:\Windows\System32\drivers\etc\hosts) to tell my client that this Web site has the IP 127.0.01. I then use the Web server to restrict the management interface to the localhost address. This not only protects my data in transit as SSL would, it adds additional layers of security.

OpenSSH Local Forwarding

To tell the SSH client to activate local forwarding, use the -L flag.

```
# ssh -L localIP:localport:remoteIP:remoteport hostname
```

If you don't specify an IP address on the SSH client, SSH attaches to 127.0.0.1. You can skip the first colon in this case, making the command:

```
# ssh -L localport:remoteIP:remoteport hostname
```

For now, only use the IP address 127.0.0.1. We'll consider binding a forwarded port to other IP addresses in "Choosing IP Addresses" later this chapter.

I use local port forwarding to connect to a remote server **pride**, that doesn't encrypt its HTTP services, adding encryption to the otherwise insecure channel. In this case, I want to connect port 80 on my local machine to port 80 on **pride**'s localhost address.

```
# sudo ssh -L 80:127.0.0.1:80 mwlucas@pride
```

I'm attaching to port 80 on the client, so I can either SSH as root or use sudo. I haven't specified a local IP address, so SSH will attach the forwarding to **127.0.0.1**. This login proceeds normally, and gives me a login on the local machine. No difference is visible in my SSH session.

If you want local port forwarding configured every time you connect to a host, use the LocalForward option in *ssh_config or $HOME/.ssh/config*.

```
LocalForward client-IP:client-port server-IP:server-port
```

This looks like port forwarding on the command line, but the middle colon is missing. Here we forward port 8080 on our client to port 80 on the server.

```
LocalForward localhost:8080 localhost:80
```

Note that this forwarding uses port 8080 on the client rather than port 80. Binding to port 80 would require using root privileges every time we SSH.

The LocalForward option most commonly appears with a Match statement.

```
Match Host pride.blackhelicopters.org pride
    LocalForward localhost:8080 localhost:80
```

When you SSH to **pride**, SSH forwards port 8080 on the client's 127.0.0.1 to port 80 on the server's 127.0.0.1. If you open multiple SSH connections to this host, however, you'll get an error on every connection except the first. The port is already bound and forwarded, so you cannot bind it again.

PuTTY Local Forwarding

PuTTY has a special control panel just for port forwarding. On the PuTTY Configuration screen's left side, select `Connection → SSH → Tunnels`. You'll see something like this.

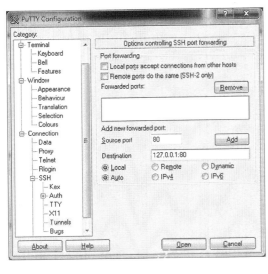

Figure 9-4: PuTTY Port Forwarding

With local port forwarding, PuTTY attaches to the client's localhost address by default. I must specify the address to bind to on the SSH server, however. To forward the local port 80 to my Web page, I bind to the server's localhost address. In Source Port, enter 80. In Destination, enter 127.0.0.1:80. At the bottom, be sure to select `Local`.

Select `Add`, then connect. Port forwarding should work. To verify this, telnet to 127.0.0.1 port 80 on the client. It should connect you to port 80 on the server.

To bind this forwarding to the client's network-facing IP address, select `Local ports accept connections from other hosts`, then connect. This will bind the forwarded port to all IP addresses on the client, so other hosts can access the forwarding. See "Choosing IP Addresses" later this chapter for a discussion of this behavior.

Figure 9-5: PuTTY Port Forwarding Settings

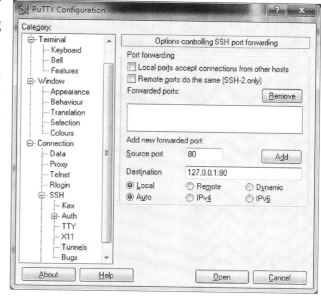

If you want this forwarding estab-lished every time you connect to this host, save the session.

Testing Local Forwarding

To verify that lo-cal port forwarding works with either the OpenSSH or PuTTY clients, connect to the forwarded service via `telnet`. Here I'm connecting to port 80 on the client, hoping to be directed to port 80 on my SSH/Web server.

```
client$ telnet localhost 80
Trying 127.0.0.1...
Connected to localhost.
Escape character is '^]'.
GET /
<html>
<head>
...
```

The Web server responds, so the port forwarding works.

Remote Port Forwarding

Before configuring remote port forwarding, verify that normal SSH works. Determine the client and server ports you want to forward to and from.

Where local port forwarding is usually used to wrap a service with encryption, remote port forwarding is used to access a service behind a firewall. For this example, I'm going to forward port 2222 on the SSH server's localhost address to port 22 on the client. When I connect to port 2222 on the SSH server, remote forwarding will redirect me to the client's SSH service.

Why do this? Remember, the client is behind a firewall. The firewall might be my home NAT device, or the industrial-grade corporate firewall cluster. Remote forwarding lets me connect to a host inside the firewall from my server on the Internet, despite any firewall rules to the contrary. This might be my emergency back door into my own network, or it might violate my employer's security policy. Or both.

Note that you cannot bind a forwarded port to SSH server's public-facing IP address unless the server is specifically configured to permit this with the GatewayPorts option. See "Restricting Port Forwarding" later this chapter.

OpenSSH Remote Forwarding

Use the -R flag to configure remote port forwarding.

```
# ssh -R remoteIP:remoteport:localIP:localport hostname
```

If you don't specify an IP address to attach to on the SSH server, SSH attaches to 127.0.0.1. You can skip the first colon in this case, making the command:

```
# ssh -R remoteport:localIP:localport hostname
```

I want to connect port 2222 on SSH server **pride** to port 22 on the SSH client, using the localhost address on both sides, so I run:

```
$ ssh -R 2222:localhost:22 pride
```

My client connects to the SSH server and gives me a command prompt. As long as that SSH session remains open, another user on **pride** could SSH to my workstation by running:

```
$ ssh -p 2222 localhost
```

Poof! A new SSH connection into the client. It's best to not have random untrusted users on the system, to prevent them from accessing external systems over your forwarded port.

If you want remote port forwarding configured every time you connect to a host, use the RemoteForward option in *ssh_config*.

```
RemoteForward server-IP:server-port client-IP:client-port
```

This looks like port forwarding on the command line, but the middle colon is missing. Here we repeat forwarding port 2222 on our client to port 22 on the server.

```
RemoteForward localhost:2222 localhost:22
```

The RemoteForward option is most commonly used with a Match statement.

```
Host pride.blackhelicopters.org pride
    RemoteForward localhost:2222 localhost:22
```

Any time my workstation connects to **pride**, remote port forwarding attaches port 2222 on the server's 127.0.0.1 to the client's port 22 on 127.0.0.1.

PuTTY Remote Forwarding

To configure remote forwarding, on the PuTTY Configuration screen's left side, select `Connection → SSH → Tunnels`. Figure 9-4 shows this screen.

As we're forwarding from server to client, the source refers to the port that will be forwarded on the server. In this case, the source port is 2222. Our destination is 127.0.0.1:22, because the client's SSH server runs on port 22. Note that most Windows hosts don't provide an SSH service. Several are available, or you might use a service such as Remote Desktop instead. I'm choosing to keep my examples consistent, and assuming I've installed an SSH server on my desktop. Select `Remote` for remote port forwarding.

Select `Add`, then connect. Port forwarding should work.

To bind this forwarding to the client's network-facing IP address, select `Remote ports do the same (SSH-2 only)`. This binds the forwarded port to all IP addresses on the server, so other hosts can access the forwarding. We consider the implications of this in "Choosing IP Addresses" later this chapter.

If you want to make the remote forwarding permanent, save the session.

Testing Remote Forwarding

Connect to the forwarded port on the server. For both the OpenSSH and PuTTY cases below, I'm forwarding to an SSH server. The connection should look something like this.

```
server$ telnet localhost 2222
Trying 127.0.0.1...
Connected to localhost.
Escape character is '^]'.
SSH-2.0-OpenSSH_5.8
```

You can now laugh at the firewall all the way to the unemployment office. Or get into your network when the VPN fails, saving your job.

Dynamic Port Forwarding

Dynamic port forwarding transforms your SSH client into a SOCKS proxy. Any traffic sent to the proxy will be sent to the SSH server, which will forward that traffic as its own routing and firewall rules permit.

For this example, I have a client behind a firewall and a server on the public Internet. I'll configure port 9999 on my client as the SOCKS server, and dynamically forward all traffic to the server for processing. I'll then point my Web browser at that port. All of my Web traffic should go over the tunnel and then onto the Internet, bypassing the local firewall and proxy server. I can test this with a Web browser.

OpenSSH Dynamic Forwarding

Use the -D flag to tell OpenSSH to use dynamic port forwarding.

```
$ ssh -D localaddress:localport hostname
```

If you don't specify an IP, ssh automatically binds to 127.0.0.1.

Here, I create a proxy on port 9999 on the local host. All traffic sent to the proxy is forwarded to the SSH server **pride**, who in turns sends it to its destination.

```
$ ssh -D 9999 pride
```

As usual with port forwarding, you'll log on to the server and get a command prompt. The dynamic forwarding runs in the background. Configure the Web browser on the client machine to use a SOCKS proxy on port 127.0.0.1:9999. It should send all traffic over the SSH session to your server.

If you want remote port forwarding configured every time you connect to a host, use the DynamicForward option in *ssh_config*.

```
DynamicForward host:port
```

The host or IP address is optional. If you give a colon and a port number, SSH will bind to that port on 127.0.0.1.

```
DynamicForward :9999
```

Like the other forwarding statements, the RemoteForward option is most commonly used with a Match statement.

```
Host pride.blackhelicopters.org pride
    DynamicForward envy:9999
```

Any time the workstation **envy** connects to the server **pride**, dynamic port forwarding provides a SOCKS proxy for everyone who can talk to the workstation.

If you've tried absolutely everything else, creating an illicit SOCKS proxy in a secure environment should suffice to get you fired with prejudice. Or you can legitimately use dynamic forwarding to access your secure environment.

PuTTY Dynamic Forwarding

Go to the SSH Tunnels menu shown in Figure 9-4. Enter a port number that your SOCKS proxy will use as the Source. Don't put anything in Destination. Select Dynamic->Add. You will see the port forwarding appear in the Forwarded Ports list. Open the connection. Your Web browser should now be able to connect via the SOCKS proxy.

For our example, I enter 9999 in the Source space, select Dynamic, and connect. That's all I need to create my tunneled proxy.

To bind this forwarding to the client's network-facing IP address, select Local ports accept connections from other hosts. This binds the proxy to all IP addresses on the client, so other hosts can access the forwarding.

Save the session if you want this forwarding started automatically every time you open this connection.

Testing Dynamic Forwarding

You can verify dynamic forwarding with any program that supports SOCKS proxies. The most common program of this sort is a Web browser, so that's what we'll start with.

Configure your firewall to block all port 80 traffic from your IP address. Verify that you can no longer browse the Web. If you're going to access the Web, you'll need to do it over a SOCKS proxy.

Start dynamic port forwarding. Modern Web browsers support SOCKS proxies. Configure your client's Web browser to access the SOCKS proxy running on port 9999, IP 127.0.0.1. (Some browsers need restarting after making such a change.) You can now access the Internet over the proxy, which means dynamic forwarding works.

Backgrounding OpenSSH Forwarding

Sometimes you want to use OpenSSH to forward a connection, but you don't really want a terminal session on the SSH server. Use the -N flag to tell ssh to not run anything, including a terminal, on the remote server, and the -f flag to tell ssh to go into the background on the client. Here, I background a local forwarding connection to the server **pride**.

```
$ ssh -fNL 2222:localhost:22 pride &
```

By backgrounding this command, you get your original terminal back. This is useful when you are not allowed to have shell access on the SSH server, but you are allowed to authenticate yourself to the server and create a tunnel. (This is one way to create an SSH-based VPN.)

Choosing IP Addresses

When port forwarding, you must choose the IP address you want the forwarded port to listen on, and the IP you want to forward that port to. Choosing the IP helps control who may connect to the forwarded port.

The most common choice is to bind to the localhost address, 127.0.0.1, on either or both ends of the tunnel. Every machine with a functional TCP/IP stack uses 127.0.0.1 as the address for itself, and only the local machine can connect to it. If I forward port 80 on my client's localhost address to port 80 on the server's localhost address, no other host can connect to that forwarded port over my tunnel. Most services on a server listen to the localhost address as well as the address attached to the network, so this is a good choice for forwarding ports from one machine to another.

If you want your client to accept requests from other machines and use local port forwarding to send them to the SSH server, attach the port forwarding to the client's network-facing IP address. If I forward port 80 on my machine's network-facing IP address to port 80 on the SSH server, this forwarding is available to all hosts that can connect to my client's port 80. With PuTTY, you must select Remote ports do the same (SSH-2 only) to attach the tunnel to your client's network-facing IP. With OpenSSH, your must have a GatewayPorts option set appropriately in `ssh_config` (see "GatewayPorts" later this chapter.)

If you want the SSH server to forward requests from other machines to your SSH client using remote port forwarding, attach the port forwarding to the server's network-facing IP address. You must adjust GatewayPorts in `sshd_config` as shown in "GatewayPorts" later this chapter. For example, we earlier used remote forwarding to connect a port on the server to the client's SSH server. You could attach this remote forwarding to the server's public-facing IP address, so that any host on the Internet could connect to the client's SSH service even though it's behind a firewall. Remember, while creating a back channel into a private network might be useful, opening that back channel to the entire Internet is downright gauche.

If you want an SSH client to act as a SOCKS proxy for other machines via dynamic port forwarding, attach the port forwarding to the client's network-facing IP address.

Suppose my desktop has an IP address of 192.0.2.18 and is on a network with half a dozen other clients. Our mail server is on another network, and does not encrypt login information. I want to provide an encrypted tunnel from my desktop to the server via local port forwarding. If I only wanted to provide this tunnel to my desktop, I would attach the client's end of the tunnel to 127.0.0.1. If I wanted to provide this tunnel to everyone on my network, I would attach the client's end of the tunnel to 192.0.2.18.

Or maybe I'm responsible for running the company's content-filtering Web proxy and I'm trying to debug a problem where a certain Web site doesn't function through the proxy. I want to see what this Web site looks like from an outside connection. I set up a private SOCKS proxy so the Web browser on my desktop can bypass the Web proxy, browsing from my server instead. I do not want my co-workers using my proxy, so I use the localhost address on my client.

You can use a machine's hostname instead of the actual public-facing IP address, provided that the hostname appears correctly in the DNS. You can also use the word **localhost** instead of **127.0.0.1**.

Also note that all IP address bindings must be chosen before opening your SSH session. You cannot add port forwarding to a live SSH session, or change the IP addresses bound during a session.

Restricting Port Forwarding

The SSH server and client control what types of port forwarding users can perform. You can entirely deny port forwarding, permit port forwarding to bind only to the server's loopback address, or permit only specific addresses or ports.

Block Port Forwarding

The *sshd_config* AllowTcpForwarding option tells sshd whether it should permit port forwarding. The default is "yes," allowing port forwarding. If set to "no," port forwarding is completely disallowed.

GatewayPorts

The GatewayPorts options control whether a client can bind a forwarded port to any server address other than the localhost. This option appears in both *ssh_config* and *sshd_config*. The *ssh_config* option controls local port forwarding, while the *sshd_config* option controls remote port forwarding.

GatewayPorts is "no" by default, meaning that clients cannot connect any port forwarding to any network-facing IP address.

If set to "yes" all forwarded ports are bound to the network-facing IP address.

If set to "clientspecified," the software will accept any configuration given by the SSH client.

Allow Specific Ports and Addresses

If you want to be more specific than GatewayPorts supports, you can restrict which TCP ports and addresses can receive forwarding with *sshd_config*'s PermitOpen option. PermitOpen takes a space-delimited list of ports that may be forwarded in the form of **hostname:port**. For example, here I permit only ports 25 and 110 to be forwarded.

```
PermitOpen localhost:25 localhost:110
```

Anything not permitted is forbidden. The SSH session will open normally, but when you attempt to pass traffic over a forbidden forwarded port your SSH client will display an error.

Now that you know how to selectively pass traffic over port forwarding, let's see how to keep an SSH session alive for hours or days at a time, without human intervention.

Chapter 10:
Keeping SSH
Connections Open

Port forwarding transforms SSH from a protocol that gets you a terminal session into a tool for arbitrarily forwarding TCP traffic. But most firewalls (and some Internet service providers) deliberately terminate TCP connections left idle for a period of time. SSH sessions left idle will eventually be disconnected by the server, the client, or some network device in between. If you're forwarding a service over SSH, or even if you just don't want to log into your SSH server every time the firewall disconnects you, you want to keep your session alive.

Most methods for keeping an SSH connection alive amount to "pass a small amount of traffic in the background so that intermediate network devices don't see the connection as idle." These are called *keepalives*. Without altering any SSH settings, running a program like `top` can simulate this – if you remember to start it every time you change to another task or get interrupted.

The problem with keepalives is that temporary disconnections will terminate the session. If your service provider has a problem in the middle of the night and the keepalive packets cannot cross the network for a few seconds, either your client or your server will terminate the connection. You must decide how to configure keepalives appropriately for your Internet connectivity. You can set two different SSH keepalives: TCP keepalives and SSH keepalives.

A TCP keepalive is part of the TCP protocol, is sent at the transport layer, and is not part of SSH itself. When a TCP connection remains idle for a length of time, it times out and disconnects. A TCP keepalive can be spoofed or forged, however. This is not necessarily bad – I can't imagine why anyone would want to spoof your connection to keep it alive, but someone more clever and nasty than I can probably come up with more than one bad reason. The time that a TCP keepalive takes to terminate the session depends on your operating system's TCP stack.

OpenSSH includes a keepalive feature that sends keepalives in the encrypted channel, making those keepalives much more difficult to forge. Additionally, SSH keepalives are highly configurable, making them less reliant on any operating system quirks.

PuTTY Keepalives

PuTTY supports only TCP keepalives. While TCP keepalives are not as configurable as SSH keepalives, they're sufficient for most end-users.

On the left side of the PuTTY Configuration screen, go to the `Connection` button. The first option is `Seconds between keepalives`. This defaults to 0, disabling keepalives. In most cases, sending a TCP keepalive every 90 seconds suffices to hold a connection open.

The OpenSSH server supports TCP keepalives by default. If you want to disable this feature for some reason, set the option TCPKeepAlive to no in `sshd_config`.

OpenSSH Client Keepalives

OpenSSH enables TCP keepalives by default. Both the client and the server use the TCPKeepAlive option to turn this feature on and off in their respective configuration files.

While TCP keepalives might meet most people's needs, SSH keepalives are much more interesting and flexible. OpenSSH supports keepalives within the actual SSH channel. The keepalive packets tell intermediary network devices that this TCP session is still in use. Receiving a keepalive tells the host that the remote end is still there, and that the SSH session is still valid. An SSH keepalive is also more likely to continue holding a session open through lower-end NAT devices.

Both the client and the server support keepalives. Strictly speaking, the client sends *client alive* messages and the server sends *server alive* messages. While these must be different for protocol reasons, to us they're just keepalives. OpenSSH doesn't use SSH keepalives by default.

A host that sends keepalives expects to receive keepalives in return. Each host keeps track of how long it's been since it saw a keepalive from the other side. If the host sends a certain number of keepalives without receiving any, it assumes that the connection is lost and terminates the SSH session.

To enable SSH keepalives, decide how often you want to send a keepalive packet, and how many of those packets can be missed before the host disconnects the SSH session. The server uses the options *ClientAliveInterval* and *ClientAliveCountMax*. The client supports the options *ServerAliveInterval* and *ServerAliveCountMax*.

The AliveInterval options specify how many seconds the connection needs to be idle before the host sends a keepalive request. To make a client transmit a keepalive after 90 seconds of inactivity, set Server-AliveInterval to 90. The default is 0, disabling keepalives.

The AliveCountMax options tell the host how many keepalives it needs to send without receiving a response before terminating the connection. The default is 3.

Let's look at how this works in practice. We have the following in the server's `sshd_config`:

```
ClientAliveInterval 90
ClientAliveCountMax 5
```

On the client side, we've put the following in `ssh_config`.

```
ServerAliveInterval 90
ServerAliveCountMax 4
```

We log into our SSH server, do some work, and let the connection go idle. 90 seconds after the connection goes idle, the client sends a keepalive to the server. If the server responds with its own keepalive, both client and server know that the connection is alive. If another 90 seconds pass without receiving a response from the server, the client will send another keepalive. It knows that it's sent two keepalive requests without receiving any response from the server. When the client sends its fifth keepalive request, after seven and a half minutes, the client tears down the SSH session and exits.

The server sends keepalives in the same way, but note that it's set to tear down the connection at 4 outstanding keepalive requests. This particular server tolerates less disconnection than the client.

Note that the TCP protocol also plays into this. A host sending TCP packets expects the recipient to acknowledge every packet. If the sender does not get this acknowledgment, it will eventually tear down the connection despite anything SSH can do. The length of time varies by operating system, but you should know that if you cannot maintain a TCP connection you cannot maintain an SSH session.

If you want to keep your connection alive no matter what, cranking AliveCountMax to high values helps, especially when you're behind a commodity Network Address Translation device such as a home router.

Keepalives and the SSH Server

If you disable all keepalives on your SSH server, the server cannot notice when a client goes offline. When a workstation crashes or a network link fails, forcibly disconnecting clients, the server won't know. It will continue running the SSH processes for those clients. I recommend using TCP keepalives at a minimum, and preferably SSH keepalives as well.

Chapter 11:
Host Key Distribution

One of the more annoying parts of properly managing SSH is distributing host keys to your users. Many users won't bother to actually compare server fingerprints to the list you provide; instead, they'll just hit "Yes, accept the key." Users accustomed to seeing scary-looking but harmless warnings learn to ignore them. (Security officers try to teach users otherwise, but user education is clearly a hole with no bottom.) One way to help users pay attention is to ensure that they don't see those warnings very often. This chapter offers ways to centralize SSH host key management, reducing your users' workload and increasing the efficacy of SSH's protections.

We'll start by covering the more flexible OpenSSH `known_hosts` file, and then discuss distributing PuTTY's key cache.

known_hosts Format

We've looked briefly at `known_hosts`, but it's time to thoroughly examine it. Every line in `known_hosts` is a separate host entry, giving the host's hostname or IP address, the encryption algorithm, and the actual public key. But each entry can also include the following fields, in this order:

- ⅄ marker (optional)
- ⅄ hostname
- ⅄ key type
- ⅄ key (containing bits, exponent, and modulus)
- ⅄ comment (optional)

Fields are separated with a space. Let's look at these one at a time.

Marker

The `known_hosts` file supports two special markers, *@cert-authority* and *@revoked*.

A `known_hosts` entry that starts with *@cert-authority* indicates that the host key is for a certification authority. Creating a central certification authority is beyond the scope of this book.

If an intruder breaks into an SSH server and copies the server's private key, that key can no longer be trusted. The systems administrator must generate a new key for the server. A savvy intruder might use the old key to try to spoof the server. By marking a key as revoked, you tell `ssh` to not accept this key on this host.

```
$ ssh pride
@@@@@@@@@@@@@@@@@@@@@@@@@@@@@@@@@@@@@@@@@@@@@@@@@@@@@@@@@@@@@
@ WARNING: REVOKED HOST KEY DETECTED! @
@@@@@@@@@@@@@@@@@@@@@@@@@@@@@@@@@@@@@@@@@@@@@@@@@@@@@@@@@@@@@
The DSA host key for pride is marked as revoked.
This could mean that a stolen key is being used to impersonate this host.
DSA host key for pride was revoked and you have requested strict checking.
Host key verification failed.
$
```

The SSH connection fails. Leaving the key on the system but marking it as revoked gives the user clear warning that the key is compromised.

Hostname

The hostname is the name the client program used to identify a specific computer. Many computers have more than one hostname, however. Computers automatically add a domain name to most requests, so a user trying to connect to the host **pride.blackhelicopters.org** might just enter **pride**. This machine might have other aliases, such as **www or mail**, and is probably also known by its IP address. To provide an authoritative *known_hosts* key list, *known_hosts* must include a key for each of these names.

The good news is that you don't have to include multiple mostly-duplicate lines for these different names. The *known_hosts* file accepts multiple hostnames in a single entry, so long as they are separated by commas. Here, we list multiple hostnames in a single entry:

```
pride.blackhelicopters.org,pride,www.blackhelicopters.org,www,192.0.2.0
ecdsa-sha2-nistp256 AAA...
```

Recent versions of OpenSSH automatically list the IP address as well as the hostname when adding entries to personal *known_hosts* files, creating entries like this:

```
pride,192.0.2.5 ssh-rsa AAA...
```

Some server administrators change the TCP port their SSH service runs on. This isn't terribly useful for security, but helps slow down the more primitive worms and reduces chatter in your logs. These hostnames appear in brackets in `known_hosts`, followed by a colon and the port number.

```
[pride]:2222,[192.0.2.5]:2222 ssh-rsa AAA...
```

In Chapter 5, we covered how you can obscure the hostnames in `known_hosts` by hashing them, preventing a casual intruder from getting server information from `known_hosts`. Listing multiple hostnames on a single line simplifies managing the `known_hosts` file, but this practice conflicts with hashing the hostnames. If you wish to hash hostnames in `known_hosts`, you must list each hostname on a separate line. A host known as **avarice.blackhelicopters.org**, **avarice**, and **192.0.2.81** requires three `known_hosts` entries. Each hostname will be hashed separately.

If a host has multiple IP addresses that receive SSH connections, you'll need to add those IP addresses to `known_hosts` as well. If you don't typically connect to all of those addresses, then don't bother. I have a server with dozens of IP addresses, but I only connect via SSH to one of those addresses, so that server has only one `known_hosts` line.

Key Type

You might see any of five different types of host key in a modern `known_hosts` file: *ssh-dss* (DSA keys), *ssh-rsa* (RSA keys), *ecdsa-sha2-nistp256*, *ecdsa-sha2-nistp384*, and *ecdsa-sha2-nistp512* (ECDSA keys). Anything else in this space in `known_hosts` is weird and should be investigated.

Key

The actual public key is a long alphanumeric string that resembles gibberish. It normally starts with a series of capital A's and often (but not always) ends with one or two equal signs (=). This fills the majority of the entry.

Comment

The comment is free-form text. You can use this for anything you desire. It frequently includes the username and machine the key was generated on. If you're using a key for automation (see Chapter 12), list the key's purpose here.

Obsolete known_hosts Entries

You might encounter a *known_hosts* entry like this.

```
pride 1024 35 12348013...
```

This key starts with a server name, two numbers, and then a key. This is an SSH-1 host key. It should never be used. Revoke or delete it.

Distributing known_hosts

All OpenSSH clients on a system check the file */etc/ssh/ssh_known_ hosts* for host keys as well as the users' personal *known_hosts*. If you create a central *known_hosts* file which contains the correct host keys for all of your servers and push it to all of your clients, your users will no longer need to manually compare host keys. They will see warnings only when host keys are incorrect. This will help them realize when there's a problem.

You must create a *known_hosts* file to implement this, however. The simplest way to prepare a *known_hosts* file is to SSH to each server and verify the offered host key against the list you've previously prepared. The catch is that you must verify all of the key types on a server. Newer OpenSSH servers support RSA, DSA, and ECDSA keys. Here, we specify which key algorithms to use.

```
$ ssh -o HostKeyAlgorithms=ssh-rsa pride
$ ssh -o HostKeyAlgorithms=ssh-dss pride
$ ssh -o HostKeyAlgorithms=ecdsa-sha2-nistp256 pride
```

It's tempting to write a simple script to collect all of these keys for all of these servers automatically, but a naive script cannot verify the host key fingerprints against the list we created in Chapter 4. If you write a script to intelligently perform the comparison, please make it available to the rest of us. Or to me, at least.

This *known_hosts* file will contain your preferred name for the SSH server and, if you have a sufficiently new OpenSSH, the server's IP address. Now get all of the server's names, both in short form and as fully qualified domain names. Ask your DNS administrators for a list of all aliases tied to this server. All of the server's names should appear at the beginning of the entry for each of this server's keys, as shown in "known_hosts Format" earlier this chapter. For my machine **pride**.

blackhelicopters.org, also known as **www.blackhelicopters. org**, I'd have a series of keys starting like this.

```
pride.blackhelicopters.org,pride,www.blackhelicopters.org,www,192.0.2.0 ssh-rsa AAA...
pride.blackhelicopters.org,pride,www.blackhelicopters.org,www,192.0.2.0 ssh-dss AAA...
pride.blackhelicopters.org,pride,www.blackhelicopters.org,www,192.0.2.0 ecdsa-sha2-
nistp256 AAA...
```

Each actual key value is different, of course. The important thing here is that each key references any host names a user might possibly use. No matter what name the user types, there's a matching key entry.

This key file is now ready for your users. Copy this *known_hosts* file to */etc/ssh/ssh_known_hosts* on all of your OpenSSH servers and clients. The next time someone uses SSH on one of these machines, the client will already have the correct key.

Installing ssh_known_hosts

Any time an SSH server's key is added, moved, or changed, users will see warnings about the host key. It's best to stay ahead of them. Update your *known_hosts* file any time you deploy or remove a server, or if you must give a server a new set of host keys. If you delay updating *known_hosts*, users will learn to ignore warnings.

The worst part of maintaining a centralized *known_hosts* file is actually copying the file to all of your servers. You are busy. If the update takes a long time or a lot of energy, you won't keep up on it. I strongly recommend using some sort of automation to install new *ssh_known_hosts* files. Software such as Puppet (http://www.puppetlabs.com), or even a simple rsync script, makes the distribution process painless. Updating *known_hosts* and distributing it to all your servers should only take a minute or two, and will save your users and your support team hours of labor.

Revoking Keys

If you have reason to suspect that a server's key has been compromised, revoke it. Add the string @revoked to the front of all of the server's public key entries in *known_hosts*. Generate new key pairs for the server and restart sshd. SSH to the server from your client to add the keys to your master *known_hosts*. Distribute the updated file to all of your SSH servers and OpenSSH clients.

Distributing /etc/ssh/ssh_config

You might find your users consistently need particular changes to their personal *$HOME/.ssh/config* files. To reduce your workload, you can set SSH client defaults globally in */etc/ssh/ssh_config*. Once you have an infrastructure to easily replicate *ssh_known_hosts* across your servers, you might as well leverage it to make helpful changes to */etc/ssh/ssh_config*. Remember that personal config file settings override system-wide settings, so a users can still shoot himself in the foot if he insists.

ssh_known_hosts vs known_hosts

The OpenSSH client checks for public keys in the users' personal *known_hosts* file, then in the system's */etc/ssh/ssh_known_hosts* file. The client will use any entry that matches the key offered by the server. Any invalid entries in a user's personal *known_hosts* will still work. It's best to move the users' *known_hosts* files to a location such as *known_hosts_personal* when deploying a centralized key repository, so that old or incorrect entries don't reduce security. Don't just delete a user's *known_hosts*, as they might well have host keys for machines you don't control in there.

Distributing Host Keys for PuTTY

PuTTY keeps its host keys in the Windows Registry. Copying the keys isn't as easy as moving a file to all of your client machines, but there are ways to simplify it. I recommend creating a *known_hosts* file for your OpenSSH clients, then converting it to PuTTY format with kh2reg.py. You won't find this script in the normal PuTTY installation file, but it's included with the source code in the *contrib* directory. Download the PuTTY source code from the same location you downloaded PuTTY from.

kh2reg.py is a Python script that reads *known_hosts* and converts it to Windows registry format. It's very simple:

```
$ kh2reg.py known_hosts > registryfile.reg
```

For example, to convert *clean_known_hosts* to the registry file *clean_known_hosts.reg*, I would run:

```
$ kh2reg.py clean_known_hosts > clean_known_hosts.reg
```

You can install this registry file on your clients with your Active Directory infrastructure or by running a login script.

If you are maintaining *known_hosts* for a variety of platforms, I suggest using the following workflow for distributing host keys across your environment. First, gather your host keys. Create a *known_hosts* file for your Unix-like clients. Trigger the script to automatically distribute the new *known_hosts* to all of your systems. While that runs, use kh2reg.py to create your Windows registry. Last, queue your new registry file for distribution via Active Directory. The next time people log in, they should have all the new keys.

Remember that PuTTY stores keys in each individual user's registry. There is no system-wide PuTTY registry tree. Distribute keys by user, not by machine.

Note that as I write this, the newest PuTTY does not support ECDSA keys. Neither does kh2reg.py; the script dies when it encounters ECDSA keys. I expect this to be fixed before you read this book. If hk2reg.py fails for you with warnings about Unknown SSH key type, remove all ECDSA keys from your known_hosts file before running kh2reg.py.

Host Keys in DNS

OpenSSH supports checking for host key fingerprints in the Domain Name System. (PuTTY does not). This eliminates pushing a file to your servers, but traditional DNS services are not secure. You *absolutely must* have DNS Security Extensions (DNSSEC) if you want to securely distribute your servers' public key fingerprints via DNS. If you do not yet have DNSSEC, go configure it now, then come back here. (DNSSEC also enables free SSL certificates for Web sites, and eventually other applications, so deploy it today.)

You should also know that the standards for SSH public key fingerprints in DNS are slowly evolving. As of this writing, there is no standard for putting ECDSA fingerprints in DNS. By the time you read this, however, I expect that the standard will appear. The OpenSSH project will certainly update its software once that happens.

We're not going to cover DNS basics. If you're considering distributing key fingerprints via DNS, I'll assume you know what a zone file is, why an RR is important, and why you update serial numbers.

SSHFP Records

The SSH Finger Print (SSHFP) record gives the SSH fingerprint for the host. The record looks something like this:

```
pride IN SSHFP 1 1 21d8f5dd6561646a3b98f0a47a6826caad68be49
```

The first field is the hostname. The second (IN) indicates this is an Internet record, while the third (SSHFP) indicates this is an SSH fingerprint. The fourth field gives the algorithm type. 1 means this is an RSA fingerprint, while 2 indicates a DSA key. The fifth field is the message-digest algorithm used to produce this fingerprint. This should always be 1, for SHA-1. Finally, the sixth field is the actual key fingerprint.

My SSH server's complete DNS record might appear something like this.

```
pride IN A 192.0.2.5
pride IN SSHFP 1 1 21d8f5dd...
pride IN SSHFP 2 1 a8533c83...
```

Creating SSHFP Records

How can you figure out all of these records? Fortunately, `ssh-keygen` will read the key files on the local server and produce the correct records. I can log into the machine **pride** and run:

```
$ ssh-keygen -r pride
pride IN SSHFP 1 1 21d8f5...
pride IN SSHFP 2 1 a8533c...
```

I copy these into my zone file and reload the zone.

You could also copy the server's public key files to your local machine and then tell `ssh-keygen` to use those files with the -f flag. You must generate records for the RSA and DSA key files separately.

```
$ ssh-keygen -r pride -f pride_ssh_host_rsa_key.pub
pride IN SSHFP 1 1 21d8f5...
$ ssh-keygen -r pride -f pride_ssh_host_rsa_key.pub
pride IN SSHFP 2 1 a8533c...
```

Remember, the public keys are displayed to anyone who connects to the server's SSH port.

Copying these files to a secured local workstation is not a security risk in most environments.

Configuring the Client

The OpenSSH client does not look for SSHFP records by default. Set VerifyHostKeyDNS in *ssh_config* to activate this behavior. PuTTY does not support SSHFP lookups yet.

Chapter 12:
Limiting SSH

We learned how to enable and disable SSH access based on username or IP address way back in Chapter 3. But what about more fine-grained restrictions? You can limit the commands that particular users or keys can run via SSH. This is helpful for very restricted access or for automated jobs. You can enforce such limits in the *authorized_keys* file or even in the SSH server itself. We'll start with the *authorized_keys* file.

authorized_keys Keywords

As discussed in Chapter 7, the file *$HOME/.ssh/authorized_keys* contains a list of public keys. When the server can decrypt a login request with one of these public keys, the server accepts that the client has the associated private key and is permitted to log in. A minimal *authorized_keys* entry has three parts: the key type, a few hundred alphanumeric characters of key, and a comment field, normally containing the combined username and hostname where the key was generated. Add descriptive comments to keys used for automation so that you can remember what they're for months or years later.

```
ssh-rsa AAAA......wC9 mwlucas@blackhelicopters.org
```

This is an RSA key. The actual key begins with AAAA and ends with wC9, and was generated by the user **mwlucas** on the host **blackhelicopters.org**. We'll use this example key for the rest of this section.

You can put additional keywords and instructions for the SSH server at the beginning of this entry. When checking the public key, the server follows those instructions (assuming the user account has adequate permissions, of course). You can find a complete list of *authorized_keys* keywords in the sshd manual page, but here are the most commonly used ones.

command="command"

Whenever someone logs in using this key, run the specified command. SSH ignores any command provided by the user in favor of the one required by *authorized_keys*. You might use this for automated processes, such as configuring a VPN (Chapter 13) or running a backup.

```
command="sudo ifconfig tun0 inet 192.0.2.2 netmask 255.255.255.252" ssh-rsa
AAAA......wC9 mwlucas@blackhelicopters.org
```

One interesting feature of providing a command is that SSH retains any command the client actually requests in the environment variable $SSH_ORIGINAL_COMMAND. You can have *authorized_keys* run a script that checks this environment variable and acts appropriately. ("The backup account is asking me to run */bin/bash*? Hello, sysadmin, we have a problem...")

environment="NAME=value"

This sets an environment variable when the key is used to log in. You can use any number of environment statements.

```
environment="AUTOMATED=1" ssh-rsa AAAA......wC9 mwlucas@blackhelicopters.org
```

By default, sshd does not permit setting environment variables. The system administrator must set PermitUserEnvironment to yes in *sshd_config* for users to set environment variables.

from="ssh-pattern"

This key can only be used for authentication if the client's address or reverse DNS matches the given pattern. See Chapter 3 for information about patterns. I frequently use this to restrict automated processes. Even if an intruder steals a private key, he cannot access the SSH server from any host other than the one I permit.

```
from="192.0.2.0/29" ssh-rsa AAAA......wC9 mwlucas@blackhelicopters.org
```

Only hosts in the IP range 192.0.2.0 through 192.0.2.7 can use this key to log into this SSH server.

Remember that reverse DNS on hosts can be forged. If you really want to restrict the hosts that can log in, stick with IP addresses.

no-agent-forwarding

This disables SSH agent forwarding (see Chapter 7) for this key.

```
no-agent-forwarding ssh-rsa AAAA......wC9 mwlucas@blackhelicopters.org
```

no-port-forwarding

This disables port forwarding (see Chapter 9) for this key.

```
no-port-forwarding ssh-rsa AAAA......wC9 mwlucas@blackhelicopters.org
```

no-X11-forwarding

This (wait for it...) disables X11 forwarding (see Chapter 8).

```
no-X11-forwarding ssh-rsa AAAA......wC9 mwlucas@blackhelicopters.org
```

permitopen="host:port"

This restricts local port forwarding so that it can only attach to the specified hostname or IP address on the local machine. If the server doesn't allow port forwarding, this has no effect.

```
permitopen="127.0.0.1:25" ssh-rsa AAAA......wC9 mwlucas@blackhelicopters.org
```

In this example we allow port forwarding to connect to our SMTP service, but nothing else.

tunnel="n"

Use a specified tunnel device for SSH tunnels (see Chapter 13).

```
tunnel="1" ssh-rsa AAAA......wC9 mwlucas@blackhelicopters.org
```

Multiple Keywords

As with just about everything else in OpenSSH, you can use multiple keywords in one entry. Separate multiple keywords with commas.

```
tunnel="1",command="/bin/tunnel.sh",from="192.0.2.8" ssh-rsa AAAA......
wC9 mwlucas@blackhelicopters.org
```

Keys and Automated Programs

Lots of us want to use SSH as a secure transport for other programs. Maybe you have a custom monitor program, or a backup process that runs over `rsync`. You don't want our client program to have a hard-coded server username and password; in addition to being insecure, it's neither maintainable nor scalable. A solution is to use an authentication key without a passphrase. By tightly restricting how that key can be used and what actions can be taken with that key, the damage an intruder can inflict with that key is minimized.

Note that the potential damage is only minimized, not eliminated. An `rsync` backup run at the wrong time can damage an existing good backup or saturate network bandwidth. Bringing a VPN up at the wrong time can change network routing in such a way that everyone will notice there's an issue. In most environments, however, these are less damaging and more visible than someone copying all your proprietary data.

First you need a user key suitable for use by a program, then you need appropriate restrictions in an `authorized_keys` file.

Authentication Keys for Automation

Automated processes cannot type passphrases. Any scheduled or otherwise automated task that requires SSH access to another host needs a key without a passphrase. Generate this key just like you would generate a host key.

```
$ ssh-keygen -f filename -N ''
```

This will create two files, one with your chosen name and one with that same name but .pub appended. Here we create a key called `task-key`.

```
$ ssh-keygen -f task-key -N ''
```

We end up with the files `task-key` and `task-key.pub`. The `.pub` file is your public key.

Either create an account on the SSH server for this automated task, or choose an existing account. The server's SSH server must permit SSH logins to that account. Install the `.pub` file to that account's `$HOME/.ssh/authorized_keys` as discussed in "Installing Public Keys" in Chapter 7.

The client machine should now be able to log onto the SSH server using the key. Remember to use `ssh`'s `-i` argument to specify an alternate key file. Here we use the key to log onto the machine **sloth**.

```
$ ssh -i task-key sloth
```

If you successfully log onto the server, the key is correctly installed. Now let's lock it down.

Developing Automation Scripts

If you're writing a script to run over SSH, you want to be certain that the script only uses the identity file you specify, rather than picking up an identity from your SSH agent. Specifying `-o IdentitiesOnly=yes` in your script's SSH command forces `ssh` to use only the identity file listed in `ssh_config`.

Limiting Automation Keys

Best practices forbid all access that's not necessary for a user to perform his task. Does the automated process need port or X11 forwarding? Turn them off. Does it need a special environment? Probably not, because you can establish that environment more easily in the user account itself. Your automated job runs on a single machine, so you can restrict the key so it can only be used from that one machine. You'll probably end up with an `authorized_keys` entry like this.

```
command="dump /home > /backups/`date +s`.dump",from="192.0.2.8",no-agent-
forwarding,no-port-forwarding,no-X11-forwarding ssh-rsa AAAA......wC9 mwlu-
cas@blackhelicopters.org
```

It's long, but tightly restricted. You don't have to worry about your backup script failing and accidentally overwriting your root partition. If an intruder compromised the host allowed to use this key and accessed this server, they could only run your backup script. That still isn't good, but it's better than the intruder stealing your data and deleting your log files.

Automation and Root Logins

"My command needs to run as root!" It is possible to log in as root with SSH. Don't do it. Logging in as root breaks many fundamental security principles in Unix-like systems. Trusting your automated script with remote root privileges is a good way to spend an unscheduled weekend restoring the servers from backup. (You do have backups beyond `rsync`, right? Remember that `rsync` is a tactic, not a strategy.) Logging in directly as root is bad medicine. It's such appallingly bad medicine, I'm not even going to tell you how to configure it. If you insist on shooting yourself in the foot with a grenade launcher, go read the `sshd_config` manual and figure it out yourself.

I readily concede that some environments can securely support root logins. Some people are securely using root logins in a manner that can support audits. If you're reading this book to learn about SSH, however, your environment is nowhere near ready for this.

If your automated process needs privileged access, use `sudo`. Sudo (http://www.gratisoft.us/sudo/) lets unprivileged users run particular commands with superuser privileges, and is available for every Unix-like system. I'm not going to go into detail on `sudo` operations; if you need a tutorial, check any number of Web sites or my own book *Absolute Open-BSD*. When using sudo to give root privileges to an automated process running as a user, you'll need a sudo configuration much like below.

```
username ALL=NOPASSWD: command
```

To give the user automation the right to run `/bin/dump /home` without a password, you might use this configuration.

```
automation ALL=NOPASSWD: /bin/dump /home > /backups/`date +s`.dump
```

Your automation user has the necessary access, and you have protected your server from intruders and automation errors. For a complicated example, we'll use these limitations to build a Virtual Private Network with OpenSSH in the next chapter.

Chapter 13: SSH Virtual Private Networks

You can wrap SSH around arbitrary TCP connections, effectively adding encryption to an unencrypted protocol. But OpenSSH also supports building generic tunnels that can pass all traffic and all protocols, not just TCP. You can link two remote offices with OpenSSH, creating a Virtual Private Network (VPN) that allows users at one office to access the other office almost as if they were on the next floor rather than the next state.

VPNs are an OpenSSH extension to the SSH protocol. PuTTY does not include VPN functions and the PuTTY developers have repeatedly stated that they do not wish to add it to their client (See the *tun-openssh* wish list item on the PuTTY Web site). We will only examine OpenSSH VPNs on Unix-like systems.

A VPN is perhaps the most complicated thing you can do with OpenSSH. This chapter assumes you've read and are comfortable with the earlier chapters, including public key authentication (Chapter 7), keeping an SSH session alive (Chapter 10), and restricting the commands available to SSH clients (Chapter 12).

SSH was not designed as a generic VPN protocol. If you have numerous client workstations that must access your private network, use OpenVPN or one of its competitors. If your sites have unfiltered Internet connections, use an IPSec VPN. An SSH VPN requires only a single open TCP port between the two sites. When you cannot use IPSec, and you only need a few clients, and you don't feel like learning a new software package, an OpenSSH VPN might serve as a quick-and-dirty solution.

Example Network

Our SSH client, **avarice.blackhelicopters.org**, has two network interfaces. One is on the public Internet. While we could refer to that interface by IP, we'll use the hostname instead. The second interface is on private network A, with an address of 172.16.0.1/24.

The SSH server, `gluttony.blackhelicopters.org`, has one interface on the public Internet. We will also refer to this public interface by hostname rather than IP address. The second network card is on private network B, and has an IP address of 172.17.0.1/24.

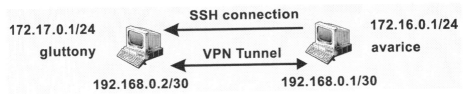

Figure 13-1: Example VPN Network

There's a point-to-point tunnel between the two hosts. The client's end of the tunnel has the IP address 192.168.0.1/30. The server is 192.168.0.2/30.

Both the client and the server run UNIX-like operating systems. We'll look at OpenBSD, FreeBSD, and Ubuntu Linux. OpenBSD has the best SSH VPN support of any operating system, and bringing up an SSH tunnel only requires editing standard configuration files. Running an SSH VPN on FreeBSD requires some basic command-line work. Ubuntu has changed parts of OpenSSH to fit better with their system, and they've also deprecated the standard UNIX networking tools in favor of Linux-specific tools. This means that we need different instructions for each set of operating systems. Among the three ways to accomplish the task, you should find an approach that works for your operating system.

Creating and managing VPNs the most difficult feature in OpenSSH, and the operating systems that support them change over time. Between the two, I wouldn't be shocked to see these VPN instructions become outdated more quickly than the rest of this book, even if you're running one of the three example operating systems. If you have trouble with the examples here, consult your operating system documentation for more current examples.

Common Concepts

The following concepts and configurations for OpenSSH tunnels appear across all operating systems. No matter which operating system you run, you must understand this material and follow these general instructions.

Tunnel Interfaces

An SSH VPN works using a tunnel (or *tun*) interface. A tunnel is a virtual interface that sits above some other network interface. The most common use for tunnel interfaces is to create a virtual link between two separated hosts, such as in a VPN tunnel. This tunnel is treated as a point-to-point connection. The method for creating a tunnel interface varies with your operating system.

When you use an SSH VPN, the client and server attach themselves to tunnel interfaces on their respective machines. When the operating system sends a packet to the tunnel interface, the packet is sent through the SSH connection. When the other machine's SSH process receives the packet, it sends it to the operating system via the local tunnel interface.

Just like any other interface you want to use for traffic, your tunnel interfaces need IP addresses. You must route traffic to the remote network to the IP address at the remote end of the tunnel. We'll see exactly how to do this in each example.

SSH Server Configuration

The `sshd_config` keyword *PermitTunnel* specifies if your client may establish a VPN tunnel. PermitTunnel has four valid options: *yes*, *no*, *point-to-point*, or *ethernet*. If set to no, tunnels are forbidden. If yes, all tunnels are permitted.

A point-to-point tunnel is a virtual private circuit that runs from one point to another. If you use a point-to-point tunnel, you must also configure routing for it to be usable. This is usually the best type of tunnel for an SSH VPN.

```
PermitTunnel point-to-point
```

An Ethernet tunnel transmits layer 2 traffic, permitting two separate locations to share their local LAN. Don't use an Ethernet VPN if you can avoid it. Local network problems on one side of the VPN can propagate across the link and saturate your external bandwidth. Configuring routing is trivial compared to the difficulties of debugging Ethernet broadcast problems from the other side of the country.

To use an SSH VPN, the SSH processes must have sufficient privileges to make changes to the tunnel devices and kernel on both the client and the server. This means that to create an SSH VPN, the SSH client must log in as root. (Changing the tunnel device owner to an unprivileged user isn't sufficient.) I stated in the previous chapter that logging in as root is bad medicine. I stand by that statement. If you're using an SSH VPN, however, you're basically out of good options. Here, we permit a root login to the client's IP address, but only with public key authentication. We also permit that IP address to open a point-to-point tunnel.

```
Match Address 192.0.2.87
    PermitRootLogin without-password
    PermitTunnel point-to-point
```

Despite what the name implies, the PermitRootLogin without-password setting allows root to log in directly only with key authentication. The root password will not let you log in.

Some older versions of OpenSSH might not let you put the PermitTunnel statement inside a Match statement. It's all right to put PermitTunnel in the main `sshd` configuration, but under no circumstances should you use PermitRootLogin outside a very tight Match statement.

IP Forwarding

For an SSH VPN to function, both the SSH server and the client must forward packets from one interface to another. This is called *IP forwarding*. IP forwarding turns a system into a router. The SSH client receives packets on its Ethernet interface, and sends packets meant for the far end of the VPN across the VPN. Similarly, the SSH server will receive packets on its Ethernet interface, and send packets meant for the other side of the VPN across the SSH connection.

VPN Authentication Key

Use key authentication with a VPN. If you are going to bring up your VPN by hand or only on special occasions, create a standard key as discussed in Chapter 7. If an automated process will start the VPN, create a key without a passphrase as covered in Chapter 12. Put the key in a separate file, rather than the usual `$HOME/.ssh/id_ecdsa`. In our example, we'll put the key in the file `~root/.ssh/tunnelkey`.

In either case, copy the public key to the server's `~root/.ssh/authorized_keys`. Verify that file's permissions as covered in Chapter 7.

This key should only be able to run the VPN commands; even with key-based authentication, you don't want a remote intruder able to get a root login on your server. I covered restricting key privileges in Chapter 12, but the exact changes to *authorized_keys* depend on the operating system.

The SSH Tunnel Command

For most operating systems, you activate the OpenSSH tunnel by running:

```
# ssh -i keyfile -f -wclientTunnelNumber:serverTunnelNumber servername true
```

The -i tells ssh which private key file to use. The -w tells the client to request a tunnel, and which tunnel device numbers to request on each side. The -f puts the SSH client into the background, so that you don't actually get a command prompt on the remote system. We run true just so we have a command that always runs successfully. You don't need a terminal window with a server root prompt lying around on your client.

In our case, the key file is *~root/.ssh/tunnelkey*. We're using tunnel device 0 on each side, and the server is **gluttony.blackheli-copters.org**.

```
# ssh -i ~root/.ssh/tunnelkey -f -w0:0 gluttony.blackhelicopters.org true
```

You'll get your command prompt back. If all works well, you won't see any errors.

Some of these command-line options can be set in the *ssh_config* file, as we'll see in the FreeBSD example later this chapter.

Debugging

If you follow the steps for your operating system and the tunnel does not start, run the SSH client in verbose mode (Chapter 5). You'll see the details of any errors. If that doesn't help, run the server in debugging mode (**Chapter 3**). Search the Internet for the exact text of your error messages. You will certainly find people who have experienced and solved these problems.

OpenSSH VPN on OpenBSD

First edit *authorized_keys* to restrict the client's access to the server. On OpenBSD, *authorized_keys* should start with:

```
tunnel="0",command="/bin/sh /etc/netstart tun0",no-port-forwarding,no-
X11-forwarding,no-pty,no-user-rc,no-agent-forwarding ssh-ecdsa AAA...
```

This ensures that even if the client is compromised, it can't do anything on the server except bring up the VPN tunnel.

Enable packet forwarding on OpenBSD with the sysctl net.inet. ip.forwarding.

```
# sysctl net.inet.ip.forwarding=1
```

To make this change persist across reboots, make the matching change in /etc/sysctl.conf.

Now configure your tunnel devices. On the client, create the file /etc/ hostname.tun0. This file contains these two lines:

```
192.168.0.1 192.168.0.2 netmask 255.255.255.252
!route add 172.17.0.0/24 192.168.0.2 > /dev/null 2>&1
```

The first line creates a tunnel interface with a local IP of 192.168.0.1 and a remote IP of 192.168.0.2. When the tunnel is brought up, the second line makes the system add a route to the remote network pointing to the far side of the tunnel. Packets to 172.17.0.0/24, the network behind the SSH server, will be routed to 192.168.0.2.

Similarly, the server needs an /etc/hostname.tun0 file like this:

```
192.168.0.2 192.168.0.1 netmask 255.255.255.252
!route add 172.16.0.0/24 192.168.0.1 > /dev/null 2>&1
```

Reboot the server and the client, then run ifconfig on each. You'll see the new *tun0* interface. If you check the routing table with netstat -nr -f inet you will see the route for the remote subnet. You cannot ping across the tunnel yet, however. Bring up the tunnel by running

```
# ssh -i ~root/.ssh/tunnelkey -f -w0:0 gluttony.blackhelicopters.org true
```

You'll get your command prompt back. If there are no errors, the tunnel is up. Ping the remote side of the tunnel. If that works, ping a private address behind the server. In our case, the server **gluttony** provides access to the IP addresses 172.17.0.0/24. If my client can ping an address in that network, such as 172.17.0.1, then the tunnel works.

OpenSSH VPN on FreeBSD

We create shell scripts to configure the VPN on FreeBSD. The client uses the script /usr/local/scripts/tunnelclient.sh, while the server has the script /usr/local/scripts/tunnelserver.sh. (Substitute your preferred script directory for /usr/local/scripts.) While scripts are not strictly necessary in this environment, using them lets me illustrate a few OpenSSH features.

Tell the server to run the script at tunnel creation by referring to it in *authorized_keys*.

```
tunnel="0",command="/usr/local/scripts/tunnelserver.sh",no-port-forwarding,no-
X11-forwarding,no-pty,no-user-rc,no-agent-forwarding ssh-ecdsa AAAA....
```

Whenever this key is used for a login, the server automatically creates the tunnel and runs the script. Even if the client is compromised and can log into the server as root, the only thing the intruder can do on the server is activate the SSH tunnel.

Enable packet forwarding on FreeBSD with the sysctl net.inet. ip.forwarding.

```
# sysctl net.inet.ip.forwarding=1
```

To make this change permanent, set gateway_enable=YES in */etc/ rc.conf*.

Now create the script to run on the server, `tunnelserver.sh`.

```
#!/bin/sh
/sbin/ifconfig tun0 192.168.0.2/30 192.168.0.1
/sbin/route add -net 172.16.0.0/24 192.168.0.1
```

When the tunnel interface appears, the script assigns an IP address to the tunnel and then routes the remote IP addresses to the client's end of the tunnel. That's all the server needs.

The client is slightly more tricky. You must enter the VPN configuration at the end of either */etc/ssh/ssh_config* or *~root/.ssh/config*.

```
Host gluttony
    HostName gluttony
    User root
    IdentityFile /root/.ssh/tunnelkey
    Tunnel yes
    TunnelDevice 0:0
    PermitLocalCommand yes
    LocalCommand /usr/local/scripts/tunnelclient.sh
```

Whenever you SSH from the client to the host **gluttony**, the SSH client uses this configuration. (When you must SSH to this server without triggering the VPN, use an account other than root.) While we covered most of these settings in Chapter 5, there are a couple of new options. The OpenSSH client has the ability to run a script on the local machine whenever you connect to another host. The PermitLocalCommand activates this feature, while LocalCommand dictates the command to run.

Whenever you SSH to this host, the client creates the tunnel device and runs */usr/local/scripts/tunnelclient.sh*.

```
#!/bin/sh
/bin/echo > /dev/tun0
/sbin/ifconfig tun0 192.168.0.1/30 192.168.0.2
/sbin/route add -net 172.17.0.0/24 192.168.0.2
```

This script starts by poking the tunnel device. The echo command won't return until the tunnel device actually exists, which prevents the script from attempting to configure a nonexistent device. It then assigns IP addresses to both ends of the tunnel, and routes the remote IP addresses to the server's end of the tunnel.

To start the SSH tunnel, run:

```
# ssh -f gluttony true
```

You'll get your command prompt back. If there are no errors, the tunnel is up. Ping the remote side of the tunnel. If that works, ping a private address behind the server. In our case, the server **gluttony** provides access to the IP addresses 172.17.0.0/24. If my client can ping an address in that network, such as 172.17.0.1, the tunnel works.

OpenSSH VPN on Ubuntu

First, edit *authorized_keys* so that the client can only bring up the VPN. The Ubuntu *authorized_keys* file should start with:

```
tunnel="0",command="/sbin/ifdown tun0; /sbin/ifup tun0",no-port-forwarding,no-X11-forwarding,no-pty,no-user-rc,no-agent-forwarding ssh-rsa AAA...
```

Even if your client is compromised, the intruder can do nothing on your server except bring up the VPN.

On Ubuntu, enable packet forwarding with the sysctl net.ipv4.ip_forward.

```
$ sysctl net.ipv4.ip_forward=1
```

To make this change persist across reboots set this sysctl in */etc/sysctl.conf*.

Ubuntu has nailed SSH VPN support to the generic interface system. To use an SSH VPN, add the following text to */etc/network/interfaces* on your SSH server.

```
manual tun0
    iface tun0 inet static
    address 192.168.0.2
    pointopoint 192.168.0.1
    netmask 255.255.255.252
    up route add -net 172.16.0.0/24 gw 192.168.0.1 tun0
```

This configuration tells Ubuntu the IP address of the interface (address), the far end of the tunnel (pointopoint), the netmask of the connection, and gives a routing command to run after the interface is operational.

The client is more complex.

```
iface tun0 inet static
    pre-up ssh -i /root/tunnelkey -MS /var/run/sshvpn -f -w0:0 sloth.blackhelicopters.org true
    pre-up sleep 5
    address 192.168.0.1
    pointopoint 192.168.0.2
    netmask 255.255.255.252
    up route add -net 172.17.0.0/24 gw 192.168.0.2 tun0
    post-down ssh -i /root/tunnelkey -S /var/run/sshvpn -O exit sloth.blackhelicopters.org
```

Before bringing up the interface, Ubuntu runs the SSH command. You'll want to substitute the path to your private key and your server's hostname. When the interface is up, Ubuntu automatically adds the route for the remote network.

How do you bring the VPN up?

```
# ifup tun0
```

To shut down the VPN, turn the interface off.

```
# ifdown tun0
```

The SSH process closes both tunnel interfaces and exits.

This concludes our excursion into SSH VPNs. Among all of these methods, hopefully you can find one that works for your operating system.

AFTERWORD

You now know more about SSH, OpenSSH, and PuTTY than the vast majority of IT professionals. Congratulations!

OpenSSH has become one of the most widely deployed pieces of security software in the world. It's included in products from Cisco, IBM, HP, Oracle, Red Hat, and more. These companies don't pay for OpenSSH. Some OpenSSH developers have their day jobs because of their OpenSSH work, and companies such as Google and GoDaddy have donated cash to support the project. For the most part, OpenSSH is created by a bunch of guys who love good software.

Running a major software project isn't cheap. OpenSSH is developed as part of the OpenBSD Project. They need servers, electricity, and bandwidth just like any other IT organization, but must constantly scrape up funding. Perhaps the most expensive, but most valuable, part of OpenSSH development is when the developers meet face-to-face. A group of programmers given one day in front of a whiteboard can accomplish more than a year of back-and-forth email across twenty-four different time zones.

If you find OpenSSH useful, consider sending them a few dollars to keep them going. See http://www.openssh.com/donations.html for details. Automatically sending them ten dollars a month through PayPal wouldn't bother most of us, but lets the developers spend more time programming and less time begging for support. If you don't want to just give them cash outright, the OpenBSD team also raises funds with a variety of T-shirts, posters, and other paraphernalia. They're handling the pre-orders for the paper version of this book to help raise funds, and plan to continue offering it as a fund-raiser. If you bought this book in electronic form, you want the paper version too. You know you do.

Similarly, the PuTTY folks accept donations. They don't have a server infrastructure to support, but they'll appreciate your support all the same. With refreshing honesty, they state that they'll spend small donations on motivational beer or curry, while larger donations can help buy any necessary hardware.

See the PuTTY FAQ for details on donations.

And if you work for one of those big companies who make a profit out of shipping OpenSSH or PuTTY with your product, please do consider getting your employer to throw a few bucks in the pot. Or at least buy some developers a few pints on the expense account. We'll all benefit.

Now go get rid of your passwords!

Made in the USA
Lexington, KY
18 March 2012